Resident Alien

Resident Alien

Feminist Cultural Criticism

Janet Wolff

Polity Press

The right of Janet Wolff to be identified as
author of this work has been asserted in accordance with the
Copyright, Designs and Patents Act 1988.

First published in 1995 by Polity Press
in association with Blackwell Publishers.

Editorial office:
Polity Press
65 Bridge Street
Cambridge CB2 1UR, UK

Marketing and production:
Blackwell Publishers
108 Cowley Road
Oxford OX4 1JF, UK

ISBN 0 7456 1250 4
ISBN 0 7456 1251 2 (pbk)

A CIP catalogue record for this book is available from the
British Library.

Typeset in 10½ on 12½ pt Sabon
by Graphicraft Typesetters Ltd, Hong Kong.
Printed in Great Britain by Hartnolls Ltd, Bodmin, Cornwall

This book is printed on acid-free paper.

Contents

List of plates

Acknowledgements

I am grateful to the John Simon Guggenheim Memorial Foundation for a Fellowship during the year 1993–4, which enabled me to finish this book; to the University of Rochester for granting me research leave during that year; and to the New York Institute for the Humanities at New York University for offering me a home during that time.

Thanks to my editors at Polity Press, Debbie Seymour and Gill Motley, for much encouragement and help; and to Polity's picture researchers, Ginny Stroud-Lewis and, especially, Thelma Gilbert, who knows much more than I do how to go about these things, and who spent a lot of time getting the necessary reproductions and permissions.

The chapters in this book were written as essays between the spring of 1990 and the winter of 1993–4, and are the product of my travels during those three and a half years. I have a lot of people to thank for invitations to visiting appointments, exchange of ideas, and opportunities to teach and work in new areas. I am grateful to friends, colleagues and students at the University of California at Davis and at Santa Barbara; the University of Western Ontario; Carleton University, Ottawa; SUNY, Binghamton; the University of Virginia; and the University of Minnesota, Minneapolis. I benefited from the advice and assistance of a number of people in the writing of particular essays, and I have acknowledged their help below. Since 1991, I have been at the University of Rochester, which has proved to be a wonderfully stimulating and friendly environment. In particular, it has been a real pleasure to work with graduate students in the Program in Visual and Cultural Studies, as well as with my colleagues in that Program, in Art and Art History, and in other departments, especially Ali Behdad, Lisa Cartwright, Douglas Crimp, Michael Holly, Ralph Locke, David Rodowick, Grace Seiberling, Tom Smith and Sharon Willis. Of these, Michael Holly earns my special thanks, for being a wonderful colleague and a good friend, and for doing a great deal to provide the circumstances in which I did much of the work for this book. I also want to thank Keith Moxey for many useful discussions about art history, cultural studies and other common concerns of ours. Thanks to Andrew Goodwin for rock music, ideas, support, and being the other reason I came to the United States; to Tony Platt for reminiscing with me about Manchester in the 1950s whenever I visit Berkeley, and for conversations about memoir and academic writing – though this book is not as personal as he would have liked; and to Mark Grimshaw and Linda Langton, for going to hear Eddie Cochran with me in Manchester on 30 March 1960, with, according to my diary, someone called Ian.

Some of the chapters in this volume have appeared elsewhere, and I am grateful to the editors and publishers for permission to reprint.

'Memoirs and Micrologies: Walter Benjamin, Feminism and Cultural Analysis', *New Formations*, 20, Summer 1993

'Death and the Maiden: Does Semiotics Justify Murder?', *Critical Quarterly*, vol. 35, no. 2, Summer 1993

'The Artist and the *Flâneur*: Rodin, Rilke and Gwen John in Paris', in Keith Tester (ed.), *The Flâneur* (Routledge, 1994)

'On the Road Again: Metaphors of Travel in Cultural Criticism', *Cultural Studies*, vol. 7, no. 2, May 1993

In addition, 'Dance Criticism: Feminism, Theory and Choreography' will appear in a collection of essays edited by Martin Kreiswirth and Tom Carmichael, to be published by University of Toronto Press in 1995.

The poetry extracts in chapter 2 from Tony Harrison's *Bow Down* are reproduced with permission from Bloodaxe and the author. The extracts in chapter 8 from Wim Wenders's *Emotion Pictures: Reflections on the Cinema* are reproduced with permission from Faber and Faber Ltd.

In respect of particular chapters I would like to make the following acknowledgements:

For chapter 2, to Andrew Goodwin, for helpful comments, for many conversations about music and for lending me his rock music books. Thanks too to Simon Frith, Mike Groden, Larry Grossberg, John Shepherd, and Ralph Locke, for comments on an earlier version of this essay. I wrote it originally for a conference in March 1990 at SUNY Binghamton on 'Feminism and Cultural Studies: Theory/ History/Experience', and I would like to thank John Tagg for organizing the conference and inviting me to it, and participants at the conference for their response. I would also like to thank Vera Zolberg and members of the Workshop on Culture and the Arts of the New School/NYU/Columbia University European Consortium, who invited me to lead a seminar in April 1993, and who made very useful comments on this essay and the one which follows it in this book.

For chapter 4, to Gretchen Wheelock and Ralph Locke for conversations about death, femininity and music.

For chapter 5, to Richard Dyer and George Dimock for comments, and to Natasha Goldman and Lianne McTavish for help with bibliographical research and visual resources. I am also grateful to participants in the conference on The Human Sciences in the Age of Theory, held at the University of Western Ontario in April 1993, who gave me useful feedback when I presented an earlier version of the paper.

For chapter 6, to Ann Braithwaite for discussion of some of these issues, to Grace Seiberling for some useful references, and to Natasha Goldman for research assistance.

For chapter 7, to Dalhousie Art Gallery, who invited me to give the lecture in November 1991 on which the chapter in based, and to those who attended and participated for their comments. Thanks, too, to seminars at the Nova Scotia College of Art and Design; the Susan B. Anthony Center, University of Rochester; Nazareth College, Rochester; the Cultural Studies Work Group at Northwestern University; Ontario Institute for Studies in Education; and the Center for the Humanities, Wesleyan University, where versions of this lecture were presented.

For chapter 8, to Ann Snitow for inviting me to give a talk, an earlier version of this chapter, at NYU, a Seminar on Sexuality,

Gender, and Consumer Culture at the New York Institute for the Humanities in March 1991. I would also like to thank the seminar members for comments and suggestions.

                                                            Janet Wolff

1

The Female Stranger: Marginality and Modes of Writing

From Penelope to the present, women have waited.... If we grow weary of waiting, we can go on a journey. We can be the stranger who comes to town.

Mary Morris[1]

The position of an outsider offers a cognitive privilege.

Leszek Kolakowski[2]

The personal is not only political, as feminists have said, but sociological and historical as well.

Wini Breines[3]

Do foreigners make the best sociologists? Kolakowski is not alone in proposing the intellectual advantages of marginality. Edward Said has claimed that one of the few benefits of the condition of exile is a certain 'originality of vision' which is the product of seeing 'the entire world as a foreign land'.[4] And there is an established tradition of sociological thought, most clearly identified with Karl Mannheim, which perceives the relatively autonomous intellectual as the more objective, and hence better, social observer.[5] The assumption is that a group which is socially unattached, or whose class (or, one could add, geographical) mobility produces a necessary relativism of vision, is in the best position to demystify the transparency of social relations and the self-evidence of ideologies. In another context, Terry Eagleton once explained why some of the best writers in the English language have been foreigners or outsiders ('exiles and emigrés'), liberated from the indigenous writer's inability to perceive the social world adequately.[6] There is, then, a certain consensus on the intellectual and critical advantages of social marginality.

But there is another point of view. If the intellectual is, potentially, the privileged social critic, this is not necessarily by virtue of outsider status. According to other theories of the intellectual, knowledge will be the product of very particular social placement – for example in Michel Foucault's concept of the 'specific intellectual' and Antonio Gramsci's concept of the 'organic intellectual'.[7] In any case, the theory that insider knowledge is inevitably partial or limited has usually been a historical observation, which blames this short-sightedness specifically on the workings of late capitalism (Fredric Jameson) or (in the case of Georg Lukàcs) capitalism after the mid-nineteenth century. I would say it is an open question (a sociological as well as an epistemological one) how much the natives can know, and not one which can be answered in a generalized formula. As for outsiders, intellectuals or otherwise, it may well be the case that dislocation makes a different understanding possible. But we must differentiate between the various types of marginality – class mobility, lack of an institutional base, exile, other kinds of geographical mobility and so on. We must also, as Said makes very clear, refrain from romanticizing exile, which is for the most part an unwelcome and often horrendous status, and be aware of the different kinds of foreign residence, some chosen, some not (exile, expatriation, immigration, travel, tourism).[8]

Here I am interested less in the cognitive advantages of marginality and more in its other productive consequences. In particular, I want to look at women as outsiders, and consider the growing evidence that becoming a stranger (for example by going abroad) is a crucial liberating step in self-discovery. (Or perhaps the point is the not-being-at-home, and not the foreign residence.) There is something about women's social disengagement that has often worked against those constraints of gender which inhibit the discovery of self (a term I hope will not be understood in any metaphysical or essentialist sense). My discussion will not be in psychoanalytic or psychological terms, though no doubt that level of analysis would be equipped to explore the topic in more depth. I am interested in the biographies of women who have 'escaped', and in the contemporary accounts of some women who have stressed the crucial importance of overseas travel and, sometimes, foreign language as a catalyst in change, in development, and, often, in literary and other forms of creativity. This kind of sociology of the marginal is not concerned with discerning positions of access to social truth or objectivity (as, for example, Mannheim was). Rather, the focus is on the sociology of creativity, and here specifically in relation to women.

But this in turn does have implications for knowledge, which brings me to the other main theme of this chapter. A new and interesting development in feminist studies in the academy recently has been the rejection of the 'academic'. I will be reading the work of women academics whose escape (often made possible by travel and marginality) has entailed a desire to address intellectual topics in a more personal mode – what the literary critics Nancy Miller and Mary Ann Caws have in fact called 'personal criticism'.[9] Here, instead of a marginality that guarantees objectivity, we have a marginality that makes possible the flight from objectivity and the integration of experience into intellectual work. Although by now the critique of 'objectivity' is well established, at least in relation to the more positivistic forms of social and natural science,[10] the matter of *subjectivity* is not unproblematic, and I will also discuss some of the issues that may be raised when ignoring the barrier between personal writing and academic writing. However, my own prejudice in this chapter, and in this book more generally, is in favour of personal criticism – of the autobiographical and the memoiristic as forms of access in cultural histories, and of the fragment or the concrete detail as a legitimate focus in social analysis.

This chapter intersects in several ways with those that follow, so that even though they were not all initially written with their inclusion in this volume in mind (apart from the first and last), their points of overlap became increasingly clear to me. Sometimes those connections seem paradoxical. For instance, here I am interested in women's travels and their positive consequences. In a later chapter, however, I discuss the obstacles to women's travel ('On the Road Again'), and in another reaffirm my earlier view that *flânerie* (another form of movement) has been a specifically male activity ('The Artist and the *Flâneur*'). I also challenge one prevalent assumption, which equates dance with freedom, especially for women ('Dance Criticism'). But I hope it is clear that I am not claiming that women do not travel, or stroll in the street or dance. Indeed, I specifically discuss the 'Victorian lady travellers' as an example of women who *did* travel – at a time when the obstacles, practical and ideological, were probably most severe. Given the gendered nature of forms of mobility (including travel abroad), I am interested, in chapter 7 and here, in how women negotiate this, find possibilities and benefit from them. In the chapter on travel (which is centrally about *metaphors* of travel), I refer to the possibilities for self-discovery by Victorian women, whose adventures on the road were impressive by any standard, but who took to their sick-beds when back in Britain.

The question of personal criticism, addressed here, also runs through later chapters. It is taken up more generally in the chapter on Walter Benjamin ('Memoirs and Micrologies'). In the chapters on popular music of the 1950s, and images of America in Britain at that time, I too engage, somewhat tentatively, in a little personal criticism ('Eddie Cochran, Donna Anna and the Dark Sister', and 'Angry Young Men and Minor (Female) Characters'), using particular moments from my own experience as a way into, in the one case, cultural theory and, in the other, cultural history. Miller refers to this intermittent use of the personal anecdote in criticism as the 'internal signature or autographics', or, taking Barthes's term, the 'biographeme' – 'the opening moves of an essay – after which the personal vanishes'.[11] Well aware of the similarly anecdotal nature of the memoiristic moments in what follows, I do not offer this book, most of which is fairly straightforwardly academic, as any kind of breakthrough into a new kind of writing. (I often think the test of this is the ability to write memoir/cultural history *without footnotes*.)

But if I may be allowed a biographeme here, I would say that this book would not have been written if it had not been for my own travels – between countries and between disciplines. I left Britain in 1988 for the United States, and spent three peripatetic years with visiting appointments at universities in Canada and the US (eleven in all, ranging from three weeks to a full semester). At the same time, I found myself increasingly in academic homes in the humanities, not sociology, my original discipline, both because of my differences with that discipline in the United States, and because of interdisciplinary moves in humanities departments of comparative literature and art history.[12] This book is the product of these journeys, not just in the sense that some of its essays originated at specific venues en route, but more particularly because new contacts, new contexts and new conversations have changed me.

So although the present chapter does not serve as an introduction to the book, and in fact focuses on a topic not discussed elsewhere in what follows, I hope that the later ones can then be read as revisiting certain themes, important to me, that are raised here.

The modern stranger

What is a stranger?

For Georg Simmel, he (and, as I will show in a moment, these texts are essentially about men) is 'the person who comes today and stays tomorrow'.[13] The stranger is 'the *potential* wanderer', whose interaction with the group is characterized by a mixture of objectivity, participation and freedom, by nearness and distance. Simmel describes this relationship as an almost entirely positive one. Alfred Schutz's stranger, on the other hand, seems weighed down by anxiety, as he tries to fathom the taken-for-granted knowledge of the group he has joined.[14] For Schutz the typical stranger is the immigrant, and his essay focuses only on the orientation of the newcomer and not on his reception or on the attitudes of the indigenous population. The strangeness of Albert Camus's stranger, of course, has nothing to do with travel or arrival or, for that matter, with social difference.[15] It is the existential strangeness of alienation from emotion and from social life. Others – philosophers and sociologists – have offered many more, greatly varied, accounts of the social condition of strangeness. On the basis of one of the most thorough reviews of this literature, Lesley Harman proposes a definition of the modern stranger as 'an inside actor with an outside glance'.[16] For her, in the end, the modern stranger is not characterized by geographical displacement (travel, arrival, immigration) or by marginality by virtue of such difference ('foreignness'), but rather by the ability to operate with the 'third-order' reflexivity employed by the ethnographer – that is the ability to distance himself[17] from the social world and at the same time retain membership. This she refers to as 'discursive strangeness'.[18]

The abandonment of the idea that the stranger is a physical intruder – literally someone who comes from somewhere else – has opened the way for sociologists to claim that in the modern world we are *all* strangers. Harman herself says that in the contemporary metropolis 'the stranger is not the exception but the rule', and that marginality (the traditional feature of strangeness) 'is increasingly a condition of modern life'.[19] Zygmunt Bauman has written about the 'universality of strangeness'.[20]

> In terms of his biography, the contemporary individual passes a long string of widely divergent (uncoordinated at best, contradictory at worst) social worlds. At any single moment of his life, the individual inhabits simultaneously several such divergent worlds. At the end, he is 'uprooted' from each and not 'at home' in any. One may say he is the *universal stranger*.[21]

With the decline of traditional society there is no need of travel to engineer strangeness and marginality if the social world in which one exists is in constant flux or no longer homogeneous.[22] This is an argument that goes back to an influential book of the early 1970s, which made the case that the modern condition for all of us now is one of 'homelessness', owing to the expansion of technology, bureaucracy and modes of abstraction, and to the pluralization of life-worlds in the twentieth century.[23] Although I am really only interested here in the stranger *as* newcomer – that is in the consequences of travel – I will say that I am wary of any claims that we are all strangers now. First, as John Shotter has recently argued, such a belief can be quite unhistorical in its view of the past as an unquestioned *Gemeinschaft*. As he says, 'we have never in fact been rooted within a single, all-inclusive order. . . . We have always been rooted . . . in the different local situations in which we live and act'.[24] In addition, we are not, of course, all cosmopolitan or even metropolitan, so that for many communities, even in the West, the world may not have been so radically transformed. There is often a somewhat conservative agenda behind these discoveries of homelessness, which tend to conclude that 'traditional family values', or at least the family, counterposed to the public world, will be our salvation.[25] I think we often exaggerate the degree of 'homelessness' and alienation in the modern world, and (the other side of this) the decline of social membership and participation in the public sphere.

I return, however, to the image of the stranger as literal (physical) newcomer. The vocabulary we use here is influenced by whether we are interested in the traveller's orientation to home or to place of arrival: the term 'stranger', unlike 'exile' or 'emigré', implies definition in relation to place of arrival. Similarly, the notion that the outsider or the stranger has a privileged point of view, from which a more comprehensive grasp of society is possible, also has two geographical references. The more common argument is that the stranger (the unattached intellectual) is well placed to understand the place of arrival – Eagleton's point about English literature (and Mannheim's argument, though not necessarily with the geographical component, about the declassed intellectual). But for Salman Rushdie the more important issue is that the writer who has left home (he is talking about India) is able to see the place of origin in a new way:

> The Indian writer, looking back at India, does so through guilt-tinted spectacles . . . I am speaking now of those of us who emigrated . . . We are Hindus who have crossed the black water; we are Muslims who eat pork. And as a result . . . we are now partly of the West. Our identity is at once plural and partial. Sometimes we feel that we straddle two cultures; at other times, that we fall between two stools. But however ambiguous and shifting this ground may be, it is not an infertile territory for a writer to occupy. If literature is in part the business of finding new angles at which to enter reality, then once again our distance, our long geographical perspective, may provide us with such angles.[26]

If the sociology of knowledge has traditionally been preoccupied with trying to identify the structural position which will guarantee truth and objectivity, the sociology of creativity (if I can so characterize Rushdie's reflections on writing) is more interested in seeing things afresh. It does not really matter whether the stranger observes the new environment or looks back at the place left behind. It seems that geographical dislocation can be the instigator of new vision and original description.

The female stranger

According to Mary Morris, quoted at the beginning of this essay, women can be strangers, too. But it is notable that, so far, all the examples taken from the literature of 'the stranger' are men.[27] Harman is the rare commentator who is aware of the implications of this, and she justifies her own use of the male pronoun throughout her book as true to the authors she discusses, who wrote before feminist critiques rendered this problematic. More importantly, it is appropriate because 'empirically speaking, "the stranger" has by and large been constructed and used as an ideal type to denote men'. The question she does not answer, but which she says needs serious consideration, is 'how is woman now implicated in "the modern stranger"?'[28] It is clear, for example, that if the stranger is, as Simmel says, the person 'who comes today and stays tomorrow', the freedom of movement this implies would work very differently for men and for women.[29] Although both women and men may be 'potential wanderers', and even actual wanderers, their conditions of wandering are very different. Like the *flâneur*, the stranger and the wanderer may be able to pass in anonymity; women, however, cannot go into unfamiliar spaces without drawing attention to themselves or without mobilizing those apparently necessary strategies of categorization through which they can be neutralized and rendered harmless. Such strategies range from finding the man to whom they are attached (so they become the wife of a traveller, rather than the traveller) to stigmatizing them as eccentric or non-respectable (because they are unattached and out of place).

In what sense, then, can a woman be or become a stranger?[30] Caren Kaplan has suggested that the displacements of the colonial and post-colonial world have produced new ways of writing and new literatures, and she emphasizes the specifically feminist impetus in this project. Considering the life and writing of Michelle Cliff, born in Jamaica and writing in New York, Kaplan says of her: 'Separated from her home and family by geography, education, and experience, Cliff articulates the boundaries between homelessness and origin, between exile and belonging.'[31] By returning in imagination to her childhood home, yet writing very deliberately from her position of displacement, Cliff is able to produce a text which 'reterritorializes',[32] and which thereby challenges notions of genre and the canon. Kaplan notes the coincidence between Gilles Deleuze's and Felix Guattari's conceptions of deterritorialization, and of a 'minor literature' (that is literature which 'moves between centers and margins') with contemporary feminist theory and its analysis of positionality. In another essay, she discusses the work of Bessie Head – born of mixed parentage in South Africa, and living in exile in a village in Botswana.

> The village became a locus for a new identity for the narrator, an
> identity forged through understanding the history of the location in

which she has chosen to live . . . Head, the outsider, became an integral part of the community in which she found herself because of the nature of the village itself. The village has gone through dramatic changes, deep divisions, and physical displacement. . . . The qualities of dynamism, change, and upheaval are not unknown to this particular author; village and writer find each other's strengths and weaknesses mirrored in this text.[33]

In both cases, she suggests that the position of outsider enables a special vision (in one case in relation to home, in the other in relation to new location). In both cases, too, Kaplan wants to argue that the search for a new way of understanding constructions of place and of history (a 'poetics of displacement')[34] is bound up with the feminist project of understanding identity and positionality, in opposition to linear narratives of the self and essentialist conceptions of gender and place. For the woman writer who is either geographically displaced (as in these two examples) or culturally marginalized ('immigrants, subjects of external and internal colonialism, subjects of racial, gendered, or sexual oppression'[35]) it may be her very identity as woman which enables a radical re-vision of home and exile.

This does not mean that it is any less difficult for woman-as-stranger to negotiate entry into a new community. But for the woman who has left home, it seems to be the case that displacement (deterritorialization) can be quite strikingly productive. First, the marginalization entailed in forms of migration can generate new perceptions of place and, in some cases, of the relationship between places. Secondly, the same dislocation can also facilitate personal transformation, which may take the form of 're-writing' the self, discarding the lifelong habits and practices of a constraining social education and discovering new forms of self-expression. This seems to have applied especially to women, and it is by no means restricted to Third World or minority women (the examples Kaplan discusses).[36] In the next section, I shall discuss the experiences and autobiographical writings of a number of First World women, who attest to the possibilities inherent in travel and relocation.[37] In doing so, I turn from my original question – do foreigners make the best sociologists? – to ask how travel affects identity and conceptions of the self. I am interested in the effects of displacement on the stranger herself, rather than on her ability to be a good social scientist.

Displacement and self-discovery

A recent full-page advertisement sponsored by Ms Foundation asks 'If all you're told to be is a good girl, how do you grow up to be a great woman?'[38] Underneath this headline are displayed photographs of eight successful and famous American women as children, each with a one-line caption recording the encouragement the girl received from her mother or father. (The advertisement then urges people – parents, aunts, uncles, grandparents and friends – to take girls between the ages of 9 and 15 to work with them on Thursday, 28 April 1994, to give them an idea of the possibilities for their own futures.) Implicit in the question is the knowledge that being 'good' stands in the way of self-fulfilment. In Western culture little girls are taught that being good is important. Carolyn Heilbrun has celebrated the successes of those women writers who have managed to break free of this, discover new identities, and express anger and self-confidence, a development she thinks is often only possible when a woman reaches a certain age: many of the examples in her study of women's autobiographical writings are women of fifty. She quotes the poet Anne Sexton, whose first serious failure to continue in good-girl mode came quite early:

> Until I was twenty-eight I had a kind of buried self who didn't know she could do anything but make white sauce and diaper babies. I didn't know I had any creative depths. I was a victim of the American Dream, the bourgeois, middle class dream. All I wanted was a little piece of life, to be married, to have children. I thought the nightmares, the visions, the demons would go away if there was enough love to put them down. . . . The surface cracked when I was about twenty-eight. I had a psychotic breakdown and tried to kill myself.[39]

Heilbrun sees Sexton as one of an important group of women poets, who were the first to have 'broken through to a realization of the narratives that have been controlling their lives' and to have expressed 'what women had not earlier been allowed to say'.[40] She does not consider the role of migration in this (Sylvia Plath and Anne Stevenson, other poets of that generation, were Americans living in England[41]), and for most of the women she discusses it was not relevant, as they stayed at home. I want to suggest a link between her notion of women 'writing a life' in certain circumstances and the idea that very often *travel* is the enabling fact. But we can certainly find examples of this before the period Heilbrun identifies as the first (namely the 'last third of the twentieth century'), starting with the Victorian lady travellers discussed in a later chapter in this book, whose journeys and writings were so crucial to the escape from the role of angel-in-the-house and to the discovery of their own desires and potential. (See 'On the Road Again'.)

In the first half of the twentieth century, a number of English and American women writers and publishers lived and worked in Paris. As Shari Benstock has shown, for most of these women, emigration was considered an escape from the constraints on women in their home cultures. For some women, particularly lesbians, it was a precondition to finding their own appropriate lifestyles. For all of them, their writing and other creative endeavours were predicated on that escape. Of women as different in background as Natalie Barney, Kay Boyle, Gertrude Stein, Sylvia Beach and Hilda Doolittle, Benstock says: 'these women appeared to share a common factor in expatriating: they wanted to escape America and to find in Europe the necessary cultural, sexual, and personal freedom to explore their creative intuitions'.[42]

> Women particularly required the freedom from external restraints, from the cultural expectations that kept women locked into social forms or placed them in the service of husbands and children and denied access to the wellsprings of their own creativity. Despite its emphasis on propriety, etiquette, forms, and politeness, France offered the perfect background for such creativity.[43]

In Benstock's account of more than a dozen such women, we perceive the intersections of their expatriation and their self-discovery.

Although Benstock suggests that there were certain features of early twentieth-century Paris which made it particularly hospitable to emigré writers, my own view is that it almost does not matter where the place of arrival is. Of course, for many artists and writers participation in an intellectual and creative community may be an essential part of discovering their own voices. In another chapter in this book ('Angry Young Men and Minor [Female] Characters') I discuss the role America (or, rather, the conception of 'America') has played for certain Europeans, including myself, who have come to associate emigration to the United States with the possibility of freedom from constraint (from having to continue to be the 'good girl'), of development and, perhaps, of creativity. And I do think there have been certain ways in which the fantasy of 'America' has operated in Britain and the rest of Europe, particularly in the 1950s, which makes sense of this notion. But I have also learned in conversation with others who have left home that, for example, California can work in such a way for New Yorkers, and even that England offers the same possibilities of escape and 're-writing the self' for some American women. This suggests to me, in another autographic reflection, that there is nothing intrinsic in the place of arrival that signifies such freedom – which is perhaps just as well, since otherwise everyone would head for the same place.

Eva Hoffman left Poland in 1959 at the age of thirteen and emigrated to Canada, where she spent her teenage years. Later, she moved to the United States, to study at Rice University in Texas, and eventually to New York, where she became a writer and editor at the *New York Times*. In her memoir of emigration and insertion into a new culture – not motivated here by the desire for self-discovery but enforced by the political situation and especially anti-semitism in Poland[44] – she records her journey into a new 'self' in the course of learning a new language. She discovers that translation does not work, because the new words do not come surrounded by the necessary network of associations.

> The words I learn now don't stand for things in the same unquestioned way they did in my native tongue. 'River' in Polish was a vital sound, energized with the essence of riverhood, of my rivers, of my being immersed in rivers. 'River' in English is cold – a word without an aura. . . . When I see a river now, it is not shaped, assimilated by the word that accommodates it to the psyche – a word that makes a body of water a river rather than an uncontained element. The river before me remains a thing, absolutely other, absolutely unbending to the grasp of my mind.

She has the same problems communicating with her school friends.

> When my friend Penny tells me that she's envious, or happy, or disappointed, I try laboriously to translate not from English to Polish but from the word back to its source, to the feeling from which it springs. Already, in that moment of strain, spontaneity of response is lost. And anyway, the translation doesn't work. I don't know how Penny

feels when she talks about envy. The word hangs in a Platonic strato-
sphere, a vague prototype of all envy, so large, so all-encompassing
that it might crush me – as might disappointment or happiness.[45]

For a while, and inevitably, English does not feel like 'the language
of the self'.[46] Later, as a student of literature, her alienation from
language stands her in good stead for grasping the willed alienation
of New Criticism and structuralism. Then, unexpectedly, after fin-
ishing graduate school, she 'cracks the last barrier between myself
and the language', while reading T. S. Eliot's 'The Love Song of J.
Alfred Prufrock'. She finds herself suddenly attuned to the sense of
the words – as she puts it, 'back within the music of language' – and
taking in the words with all their complexity of meaning and association. By the end of her story, she realizes that she talks to herself
in English and also that, because English is the language in which
she has grown to adulthood, Polish cannot cover much of her experience.[47] Unlike other women's stories of travel, 'foreignness' and
self-discovery, Hoffman's is pervaded by an elegiac sense of her
original loss of home. It is a narrative of struggle in another language and culture (though it is also simply a record of the normal
agonies of adolescence). Yet the adult she has become is the woman
who begins to write, whose successful career as a writer can only be
seen as the product of her trials with language and translation.

Alice Kaplan's relationship with another language was altogether
more enthusiastic. From very early on, growing up in the American
mid-West, she knew that French, and France, would be her salvation.
She went to school for a year in Switzerland, dedicatedly improving
her French, and delirious with happiness when she finally got the
French 'r' right.[48] 'Living in French', she even found that she was
good at sports, where at home she had been the worst; here again,
she says, 'French had saved me'.[49] Later, as a college student of French
on her junior year abroad in Paris, a love affair seemed to be mainly
defined by how French she can learn to become from the man involved, a project which had limited success. 'I wanted to breathe in
French with André, I wanted to sweat French sweat. It was the
rhythm and pulse of his French I wanted, the body of it, and he
refused me, he told me I could never get that. I had to get it another
way.'[50] And so her adventures in French, and in France, continued.
If she is aware that she used French as somewhere to hide, she also
records her absolute dependence on it in her own development.

Learning French and learning to think, learning to desire, is all mixed up in my head, until I can't tell the difference. French is what released me from the cool complacency of the R Resisters, made me want, and like wanting, unbuttoned me and sent me packing . . . French got me away from my family and taught me how to talk. Made me an adult. And the whole drama of it is in that 'r', how deep in my throat, how different it feels.[51]

As other women have found, cultural and physical distance from home made possible for her both self-discovery and writing.

Writing and marginality – fragments and memoirs

In the acknowledgements at the end of her book, Alice Kaplan tells the reader that she began work on *French Lessons* in a writing group which had been meeting since 1987 in Durham, North Carolina. An excerpt from it was published in the journal *Lingua Franca* before the book appeared, with an introduction describing it as 'an experiment in autobiography', in which Kaplan, with the other members of the writing group, 'tried out subjective approaches to academic prose'.[52] It is a memoir, not an academic book; yet throughout the entire second half of the text the life-history is closely entwined with Kaplan's research obsessions, teaching concerns and academic interests as a professor of French literature. Indeed, an unusual and important aspect of the book is that it records how an academic career can grow *out of* personal experiences. Thus, as we read the memoir we perceive a link between Kaplan's memory of her father (who had been a prosecutor at the Nuremberg trials and who died when she was eight) and her own eventual fascination with French fascist writers and intellectuals – first Céline, and later Maurice Bardèche. We understand that her current life and work is very clearly the consequence of her earlier need to use French as both an escape and a route to self-discovery. So, for example, her reflections on post-structuralist theory and on Paul de Man are inseparable from her own relation to language(s) and, through her father, and as Jewish herself, to anti-semitism. In all of this we are also made to see that issues which are normally presented as purely academic matters are more than likely to originate in, and remain connected with, biographical and subjective concerns.

This realization resonates with a growing feeling, especially among some feminist critics, that the separation of the academic and the personal is not only artificial, but also damaging. Jane Tompkins (another member of Kaplan's reading group) produced an early manifesto to this effect, declaring war on the injunction to keep experience out of literary–critical writing. 'The criticism I would like to write would always take off from personal experience. Would always be in some way a chronicle of my hours and days. Would speak in a voice which can talk about everything, would reach out to a reader like me and touch me where I want to be touched.'[53] Such writing would not risk alienating either author or reader in the way, Tompkins finds, most academic texts do. (Guattari, Harold Bloom, and Foucault fail her test here; a feminist anthology on desire and erotic domination, on the other hand, engages her full attention.[54]) This alienation, in the name of objectivity, she perceives as an aspect of patriarchy, and hence the reconnecting of writing and the self becomes a feminist project.[55] This project is joined explicitly (though with some minor disagreements with Tompkins) by Miller in her own commitment to 'personal criticism'.[56] And other women have been reflecting on the connection between the personal and the academic in general, and on their relationship to their own scholarship.[57] Apart from Alice Kaplan, no one faces the possibility that this new kind of writing might have been made possible by a position of marginality or by geographical displacement, and it may not always be relevant. (But it is worth mentioning that Miller, too, has worked on French, in French, and in France; she calls herself 'a recovering francophile'.[58]) Travel, of course, is not the only route to self-reflection and distance, and it would be interesting to discover what other biographical events motivated the desire for personal criticism in writers who have remained mono-cultural. I want to retain the connection, however, because I believe that cultural (linguistic, geographical) marginality *is one important factor* which enables self-discovery. For some women academics, this release of what Sexton called the 'buried self' has led to a rejection of those models of distance and objectivity in which they were trained, and to the beginnings of an attempt to render visible the threads which connect experience and biography with intellectual work.

This move towards the memoiristic is not without its difficulties. Joan Scott has challenged the reference to experience in historical work, on the grounds that it is 'foundational' – that it is premised on the existence of preconstituted subjects, and hence 'preclude(s) inquiry into processes of subject-construction'.[59] But, as noted in the next chapter, I do not see this is a problem, for two reasons. In the first place, even though subjectivity is constructed, not given, and moreover always in flux, it is not the only task of historical and critical accounts to address this construction. Secondly, it may be that even in starting from experience – our own or that of a historical subject – we are able to explore its discursive and social construction. In other words, a methodological focus on subjectivity does not entail a commitment to essentialism. Linda Kauffman's two-part objection to the use of personal testimony in critical practice is different but also, I think, not really damaging to the project I have been considering. Acknowledging that 'our intellectual work as feminists is directly related to our personal histories; that our subjective experiences influence our politics, that our psychic traumas affect our teaching and writing', Kauffman nevertheless speaks against the tendency to base criticism on the personal.[60] Her central argument is a political one: that Tompkins and others who advocate personal testimony risk substituting individualism for a collective feminist politics. As Kauffman puts it, 'Writing about yourself does not liberate you, it just shows how ingrained the ideology of freedom through self-expression is in our thinking.'[61] However, while this would be a problem for feminist politics, it is not necessarily one for cultural criticism and social history, whose intentions are not mobilization, but analysis.

Kauffman's second point is that we cannot simply regard the personal as inherently paradigmatic.[62] Both Tompkins and Miller acknowledge that the personal might, in the end, be *just* personal. But here, I think, the issue is not the legitimacy of *subjectivity* in academic writing, but the problem of assuming *typicality* for any kind of evidence. In other words, what is at issue is whether the fragment – the memory, the concrete instance – can be said to stand for something beyond itself, to be somehow typical of a moment in cultural history. (I address this question in a later chapter.[63]) And it is not possible to give a generic answer, since sometimes the particular may be quite idiosyncratic, and lead nowhere; at other times, it may, like Benjamin's 'dialectical image', encapsulate important aspects of the social and political moment. Whether the concrete instance is an experience or an objectively described phenomenon, the question of typicality has to be decided by the reader or by other cultural and social historians. In the case of memoir and the subjective, the particular selectivity involved in recall may seem to be a drawback. But we should also be aware of the productive aspects of forgetting, recognized by Salman Rushdie: '[Of] course I'm not gifted with total recall, and it was precisely the partial nature of these memories, their fragmentation, that made them so evocative for me. The shards of memory acquired greater status, greater resonance, because they were *remains*; fragmentation made trivial things seem like symbols, and the mundane acquired numinous qualities.'[64] The narrative constructed from personal testimony, from fragments of memoir, and from apparently isolated moments, competes on equal terms with other narratives, including those formulated in macro-sociological or abstract terms. My suggestion is that the narrative of the fragment and the memoir, motivated as it is by those who have reclaimed their 'buried selves', often in the process of a journey, is one worth telling.

On having a green card

It will probably be clear that this book, as its title suggests, is really about my own success in attaining a particular category of 'strangeness'. Having had my fingerprints taken at Rochester police station, my right ear photographed at the accredited studio and my blood extracted to establish HIV status, I drove to Buffalo in a snowstorm in March 1992 for my interview with the Immigration Service, and came back a Resident Alien. By then, my own period of travels was (for the moment) over. The chapters that follow are somehow the product of those travels, most of them written since that date. Though they were written for different occasions (most of them originally as lectures, two for publication in other volumes) they have in common certain persistent themes: gender and mobility (travel, dance, *flânerie*), memoir and social history, the fragment and the concrete in cultural theory.

In the end, I do not suppose it is true that foreigners necessarily make the best sociologists, though I do think displacement provides unique opportunities for new vision. What is true is that there are other, equally important, reasons for women to travel. Barred though they may be from the classic role of the stranger, women can nevertheless take advantage of the many opportunities to 'go on a journey', as Morris puts it, and in so doing to begin the essential process of transforming and discovering themselves.

NOTES

1 Mary Morris, *Maiden Voyages: Writings of Women Travelers* (Vintage Books, 1993), p. xxii.
2 Leszek Kolakowski, 'In praise of exile', in *Modernity on Endless Trial* (University of Chicago Press, 1990), p. 57.
3 Wini Breines, *Young, White, and Miserable: Growing Up Female in the Fifties* (Beacon Press, 1992), p. x.
4 Edward Said, 'Reflections on exile', *Granta* vol. 13 (Autumn 1984), pp. 171–2.
5 Karl Mannheim, 'The prospects of scientific politics', in *Ideology and Utopia* (Routledge & Kegan Paul, 1960 [1936]), especially pp. 136–46.
6 Terry Eagleton, *Exiles and Emigrés: Studies in Modern Literature* (Schocken Books, 1970). Eagleton's thesis is indebted to Perry Anderson's famous essay, 'Components of a national culture', *New Left Review*, no. 50 (July–August 1968), which argued that many of the most important contributions to English culture came from immigrants. However, there are obviously shades of Lukàcs here too (the notion of position as enabling perception of the social totality), and similarities with Fredric Jameson's argument, in numerous essays, that inhabitants of capitalist society at a particular historical moment lose the ability to understand the society as a whole. For Eagleton, of course, as for Lukàcs, the assumption is that good literature *is* that which represents society adequately.
7 Michel Foucault, 'Truth and power', in *Power/Knowledge: Selected Interviews and Other Writings, 1972–1977* (Harvester Press, 1980), p. 126. See also his 'Intellectuals and power', in *Language, Counter-Memory, Practice: Selected Essays and Interviews* (Basil Blackwell, 1977). Antonio Gramsci, 'The formation of intellectuals', in *The Modern Prince and Other Writings* (International Publishers, 1959). See also R. Radhakrishnan, 'Toward an effective intellectual: Foucault or Gramsci?', in Bruce Robbins (ed.), *Intellectuals: Aesthetics, Politics, Academics* (University of Minnesota Press, 1990).
8 I discuss the romanticization of exile in the chapter on Walter Benjamin, 'Memoirs and Micrologies', in this volume.
9 Nancy K. Miller, 'Getting personal: autobiography as cultural criticism', in *Getting Personal: Feminist Occasions and Other Autobiographical Acts* (Routledge, 1991). Mary Ann Caws, 'Personal criticism: a matter of choice', Ch. 1 of *Women of Bloomsbury* (Routledge, 1990).

10 Amongst other things, I refer here to the work of sociologists and philosophers of science, who have exposed the very *non*-scientific procedures of scientific enquiry; the so-called 'new ethnography', which has demonstrated the dialogic nature of knowledge, and the implication of the ethnographer in his or her enquiry and, hence, its results; the realization (after hermeneutics, semiotics and theories of narrative) that all knowledge is interpretation; and the recognition, thanks to the sociology of knowledge and the critical theory of the Frankfurt School, that all knowledge is socially grounded and represents particular interests.

11 Miller, 'Getting personal', pp. 2 and 26 (note 2).

12 I discuss these developments at greater length in the Afterword to the second edition of my book, *The Social Production of Art* (Macmillan, 1993 [1981]).

13 Georg Simmel, 'The stranger', in Kurt H. Wolff (ed.), *The Sociology of Georg Simmel* (Collier-Macmillan, 1950), p. 402.

14 Alfred Schutz, 'The stranger: an essay in social psychology', in *Collected Papers* vol. II: *Studies in Social Theory* (Martinus Nijhoff, 1964).

15 Albert Camus, *The Stranger* (Vintage Books, 1988 [1942]). Racial difference, between Arab and French-Algerian, is not the issue in the novel.

16 Lesley Harman, *The Modern Stranger: On Language and Membership* (Mouton de Gruyter, Berlin, 1988), p. 7.

17 Again, Harman makes clear early in her book that her model of the stranger is gendered male.

18 Harman, *The Modern Stranger*, p. 155.

19 Ibid., pp. 44 and 93.

20 Zygmunt Bauman, 'Strangers: the social construction of universality and particularity', *Telos*, no. 78 (Winter 1988–89), p. 36.

21 Ibid., p. 37.

22 However, George Steiner also believes that universal mobility is part of the modern condition in what he calls 'the age of the refugee'. For him the 'homelessness' is as much physical as social and existential. George Steiner, *Extraterritorial: Papers on Literature and the Language Revolution* (Penguin, 1975), p. 21.

23 Peter L. Berger, Brigitte Berger and Hansfried Keller: *The Homeless Mind: Modernization and Consciousness* (Random House, 1973).

24 John Shotter, 'Rhetoric and the roots of the homeless mind', *Theory, Culture & Society*, vol. 10, no. 4 (1993), p. 42.

25 Berger et al. do conclude this. See also Christopher Lasch, *Haven in a Heartless World: The Family Besieged* (Basic Books, 1979).

26 Salman Rushdie, *Imaginary Homelands: Essays and Criticism 1981–1991* (Granta Books, 1991), p. 15.

27 All the writers discussed in Eagleton's *Exiles and Emigrés* are men too: Joseph Conrad, Evelyn Waugh, George Orwell, Graham Greene, T. S. Eliot, W. H. Auden and D. H. Lawrence.

28 Harman, *The Modern Stranger*, p. 9, n. 2.

29 Here I am making more or less the same argument I made in an earlier essay about the *flâneur*, and which I take up later in this volume in 'The Artist and the *Flâneur*'. See my article 'The invisible *flâneuse*: women and the literature of modernity', *Theory, Culture & Society*, vol. 2, no. 3 (1985), reprinted in my *Feminine Sentences: Essays on Women and Culture* (Polity Press, 1990).

30 Lou Andreas-Salomé maintained that women were never 'homeless', but remained 'at home' in exile because, as Biddy Martin paraphrases her, woman 'carried a sense of home around with her, as a snail carries its shell on its back wherever it wanders'. Biddy Martin, *Woman and Modernity: The (Life)Styles of Lou Andreas-Salomé* (Cornell University Press, 1991), p. 43.

31 Caren Kaplan, 'Deterritorializations: the rewriting of home and exile in western feminist discourse', *Cultural Critique* no. 6 (Spring 1987), p. 195.

32 The term, together with its counterpart 'deterritorialization', is taken from the work of Gilles Deleuze and Felix Guattari, especially 'What is a minor literature?', in *Kafka: Towards a Minor Literature* (University of Minnesota Press, 1986).

33 Caren Kaplan, 'Reconfigurations of geography and historical narrative: a review essay', *Public Culture*, vol. 3, no. 1 (Fall 1990), p. 30. The text referred to is Bessie Head's non-fiction work, *Serowe: Village of the Rain Wind* (Heinemann, 1981).

34 Kaplan, 'Reconfigurations of geography and historical narrative', p. 26.

35 Kaplan, 'Deterritorializations', p. 190.

36 She also discusses the white American writer, Minnie Bruce Pratt, however, marginalized in southern US culture by her lesbianism and non-southern life-style: 'Deterritorializations'.

37 In turning from all those male 'exiles and emigrés' to women, I do not want to claim that it is *only* women who 're-write the self' as a result of geographical displacement. Keya Ganguly's study of a group of middle-class immigrants to the United States from India shows how both men and women in that community used memories of home to 'reinvent the past and themselves', though in different ways. Keya Ganguly, 'Migrant identities: personal memory and the construction of selfhood', *Cultural Studies*, vol. 6, no. 1 (1992). The quotation is from p. 41.

38 *New York Times*, Thursday, 20 January 1994.

39 Anne Sexton, *A Self-Portrait in Letters*, eds Linda Gray Sexton and Lois Ames (Houghton Mifflin, 1977), pp. 399–400, quoted in Carolyn G. Heilbrun, *Writing a Woman's Life* (W. W. Norton, 1988), p. 70.

40 Heilbrun, *Writing a Woman's Life*, p. 60.

41 See Janet Malcolm's essay on Plath, in which Stevenson also figures importantly: 'Annals of biography: the silent woman', *New Yorker* (August 23 and 30, 1993).

42 Shari Benstock, *Women of the Left Bank: Paris, 1900–1940* (Virago, 1987), p. 10.

43 Ibid., p. 78.

44 For a thirteen-year-old girl, this leaving was painful and unwelcome. Indeed, the chapter of her book which deals with her early life in Poland is entitled 'Paradise'. Eva Hoffman, *Lost in Translation: A Life in a New Language* (Penguin, 1989).

45 Ibid., pp. 106, 107.

46 Ibid., p. 121.

47 Ibid., pp. 183, 186, 272.

48 Alice Kaplan, *French Lessons: A Memoir* (University of Chicago Press, 1993), p. 55.

49 Ibid., p. 57.

50 Ibid., p. 94.

51 Ibid., pp. 140–1, 216.

52 Alice Kaplan, 'Out of the past: encounters with a French collaborationist', *Lingua Franca* (September/October 1993), p. 34.

53 Jane Tompkins, 'Me and my shadow', in Linda Kauffman (ed.), *Gender and Theory: Dialogues on Feminist Criticism* (Basil Blackwell, 1989), p. 126. An earlier version of the essay was published in *New Literary History*, vol. 19 (1987).

54 Ann Snitow, Christine Stansell and Sharon Thompson (eds), *The Powers of Desire: The Politics of Sexuality* (Monthly Review Press, 1983).

55 It is not only women, however, who have made the move towards subjective criticism. The work of some men, particularly in anthropology, has considered the role of experience in academic work. See Michael Jackson: *Paths toward a Clearing: Radical Empiricism and Ethnographic Inquiry* (Indiana University Press, 1989); Renato Rosaldo, 'Introduction: grief and a headhunter's rage', in *Culture and Truth: The Remaking of Social Analysis* (Beacon Press, 1989). Acknowledging the role of the subjective, however, is more often a recommendation for a better methodology than a political or personal value in such cases.

56 Miller, 'Getting personal'.

57 See, for example, Susan Rubin Suleiman, 'War memories: on autobiographical reading', *New Literary History*, vol. 24, no. 3 (1993); Ann Snitow, 'A gender diary', in Marianne Hirsch and Evelyn Fox Keller (eds), *Conflicts in Feminism* (Routledge, 1990). Also, see the collection of essays addressing 'the process by which women scholars became feminist scholars, articulating the connections between the personal and the political in their lives and work': Gayle Greene and Coppélia

Kahn (eds), *Changing Subjects: The Making of Feminist Literary Criticism* (Routledge, 1993).

58 Nancy K. Miller, 'The French mistake', in *Getting Personal*, p. 48. See also the personal French connection for Naomi Schor in her '*Cartes postales*: representing Paris 1900', *Critical Inquiry*, vol. 18 (1992).

59 Joan W. Scott, 'The evidence of experience', *Critical Inquiry*, vol. 17, no. 4 (1991), p. 783.

60 Linda S. Kauffman, 'The long goodbye: against personal testimony or, an infant grifter grows up', in Greene and Kahn (eds), *Changing Subjects*, p. 130.

61 Ibid., p. 139.

62 Ibid., p. 133.

63 'Memoirs and Micrologies'.

64 Rushdie, *Imaginary Homelands*, pp. 11–12.

2

Eddie Cochran, Donna Anna and the Dark Sister: Personal Experience and Cultural History

On Sunday, 17 April 1960, the American rock 'n' roll singer Eddie Cochran was killed in a car accident near Bath. He was on his way to London Airport, to fly home for a short break in the middle of a successful tour. Gene Vincent, on tour with him, was injured in the accident. Unlike Don McLean, whose 1971 song 'American Pie' fixes 3 February 1959 (the day of the plane crash which killed Buddy Holly, Ritchie Valens and the Big Bopper) as *the* tragic moment in the history of rock 'n' roll ('the day the music died'), I would insist instead, in terms of my own personal music history, on that Easter Sunday in 1960. Music did not finally die until 11 December 1964, the day Sam Cooke was shot and killed by the woman manager of a motel in Los Angeles. Earlier that year, the Rolling Stones had their first No. 1 hit in Britain, with the song 'It's All Over Now'. And, apart from the Rolling Stones themselves, it was.[1]

The *Rolling Stone History of Rock & Roll* describes the death of Eddie Cochran in a chapter entitled 'The Dark Ages'.[2] Like those ideologically distorted histories of art and ideas that employ this phrase to write off the centuries between the cultures of Greece and Rome and that of the early Renaissance, a certain historical orthodoxy lies behind this notion in rock history. The first great moment of rock 'n' roll is identified as the short period between 1955 (the year Bill Haley's 'Rock around the Clock' was the first rock 'n' roll song to become a No. 1 hit[3] and the year of Elvis Presley's first national hits in the United States) and 1958 (the year Elvis went into the army). The charts in the following years were dominated by 'teen-idol' music, bland ballads and country-and-western hits. Rock music's image was damaged by the payola scandals of 1959 and 1960, Jerry Lee Lewis's marriage to his 14-year-old cousin, Chuck Berry's conviction on a charge of transporting a minor across state lines for immoral purposes, Elvis's absence in the army for two years, and the deaths of Buddy Holly, the Big Bopper and Eddie Cochran. One rock history book concludes its account of music in 1959 like this: 'And just in case anybody was still feeling good, *Billboard's* December 14 issue had even more bad news: "The Chipmunk Song" had reentered the charts for the second year in a row, and was on the Hot 100 at number 89. Somebody call an exterminator!'[4] The so-called 'Renaissance' which ended this period of darkness was the 'British Invasion', which began with the Beatles' first US tour in 1964. British groups took over the charts in both Britain and the United States (on 21 March 1964, for the first time, all the Top Ten singles in Britain were by British acts[5]), and the new music opened the way for acid rock, progressive rock and other counter-cultural forms.

This orthodoxy does not bear much relation to my own music history. It was not that I was entranced by American hits like Johnny Tillotson's 'Poetry in Motion' or Bobby Vee's 'Rubber Ball'. To that extent, I too think of those years around 1960 as 'the dark ages'. But from the point of view of a rock fan in Britain in the early 1960s, the take-over of music by the British groups was (with a couple of exceptions) a disaster. It did more than any moralizing politicians or censoring broadcasters could do to obliterate the excitement and the possibilities awakened by early rock 'n' roll. The arrival of British music produced real gains: a new sophistication in popular music, originality and variety in lyric-writing, complexity in composition and (sometimes) orchestration, and new standards of virtuosity in technique – the kinds of thing which have made post-rock 'n' roll musicians fit subjects for serious study by musicologists.[6] The loss is more difficult to define,[7] but has to do with the *beat*, the *voice* and the *body*. As Paul Willis shows, English bikers in the late 1960s understood this:

> It is in the light of the 'golden age' and its cultural resonance for the motor-bike boys that we can understand their attitudes to later artists.

> The Beatles' albums *Revolver* and *Sergeant Pepper* were immensely
> successful records, but they had clearly deserted the spirit of early
> rock 'n' roll. With their melodic asymmetry and complexity of rhythm,
> they had an authenticity of their own, but it was not the authenticity
> of the 'big beat', rock 'n' roll era. . . . The Rolling Stones . . . whom
> the boys consistently rated highly, can be seen as giving a rebirth in
> the 1960s to the rock 'n' roll of the mid-1950s. The Stones' music
> began with strong simple rhythms and conventional chord patterns
> and metre taken fairly directly from Chicago rhythm and blues.[8]

As he says, one of the most noticeable things about the music the
bike boys favoured was the prominence of its beat: 'it is music for
dancing to' (p. 67). Trent Hill, too, stresses the importance of the
'powerful, pulsing beat' of early rock 'n' roll music,[9] a central aspect
of its origins in rhythm and blues (rock being a hybrid of r & b,
blues and country music). The beat implicates, and is experienced
in, the body; as Lawrence Grossberg puts it, 'rock and roll is corporeal and "invasive"'.[10] And the connection of the body and sexual
expression has always been a central part of the campaign against
rock music.[11] David Buxton explains both the connection and the
reaction:

> The undisciplined consumer body was defined in part by the functional
> relation between music and dance in rock music, a relation enhanced
> by rhythmic borrowings from the blues and jazz; the sexual freedom
> widely accepted to be inherent in the music and dance of American
> blacks provided an apparently liberating element: eroticism. Rock
> music could be said to have given back to middle-class whites their
> bodies.[12]

The voice of the singer is also crucially important here, as rock 'n'
roll reproduces the tone and the style of blues and r & b singers.[13]
Simon Frith identifies the appeal of Elvis Presley in 'the grain of his
voice'.[14] Andrew Chester quotes Eddie Cochran himself on this: 'In
rock 'n' roll the beat is only supplementary to the human voice. It's
the voice, coupled with an extraordinary sense of emotion, which
lends to rock 'n' roll a personality not sensed in other types of
music.'[15]

The roots of early rock 'n' roll in black music are clear in the case
of American music, a fact which has raised some important questions:
issues of expropriation and exploitation (because white singers found

success with the music and songs of black musicians); questions about origin and authenticity;[16] and notions of transgression, which suggest the doubly subversive nature of this music in crossing boundaries of race. But the case of Britain was different. Immigration on a large scale from Africa and especially the Caribbean did not begin until the 1950s. Nor was there an indigenous black musical culture that was appropriated for rock. As Alan Sinfield points out, 'in Britain the Black dimension of rock-'n'-roll was relatively unappreciated'.[17] The music was an import from the United States, and it signified 'American' rather than 'black'. In fact, little of the music of black musicians was available in Britain, and access to American rock 'n' roll in general was fairly limited.[18] The dimension of race in the culture of rock music in Britain in the 1950s is not evident, but it was certainly not foregrounded in the way it was in the United States.

I have been talking as though the appeal of rock 'n' roll (of Eddie Cochran) is simply *there*, in the music – in the beat, the body and the voice. Work on youth culture has shown, of course, that music, like other aspects of fashion and style, operates in conjunction with a complex process of the formation of individual and social identities, and may therefore in some sense be selected on the basis of affective criteria other than the sound itself.[19] In addition, the evidence of responses by other listeners seems to work against any suggestion that a song or a singer has a self-evident meaning or appeal. One question rock critics have often raised is whether rock 'n' roll, with its phallic beat and masculinist culture, can or *should* appeal to women.[20] Sue Wise, reflecting on her period as an Elvis fan, feels obliged to justify his appeal by rejecting Elvis the 'butch god' (an image, she says, constructed by men) in favour of Elvis 'the teddy bear' – a 'private, special friend' to a lonely adolescent (an appreciation of the King which is probably at least partly explained by the facts that she was born in 1953 and that her fandom relates to the period of his decline into a Las Vegas ballad singer).[21] She does not discuss the music at all or make it clear which of Elvis's songs (or periods) she prefers, which suggests that they are *not* the rock numbers. But there is also a way in which the music of your teens is *your* music. If I had been 15 in 1967, or 1976, it is likely my identification would have been with Jefferson Airplane, or with punk rock, and I might well think that the music of a later time was in some ways a sell-out. I do believe that for those who were in their teens in the late 1950s there was a coincidence of personal history and cultural history, in which the emergence of rock 'n' roll and the development of the first youth cultures (clothes, records, coffee bars, style, leisure) produced and reinforced the sense of identity, separation and liberation of young adulthood.[22]

So I do want to argue that there is something in the music of early rock 'n' roll which constitutes a direct appeal – to the body, to the emotions. I am aware of the dangers of proposing anything like essential characteristics (indeed, I argue strongly against this in another chapter in this book[23]), and yet I think it is the case that certain rhythms, certain musics, simply involve the body.[24] The best rock music combined the intensity of the persistent beat with the power and rawness of the blues voice. Eddie Cochran, in songs like 'C'mon Everybody'[25] (described by Dave Marsh as the 'greatest party invitation of the rock and roll era'[26]), achieved just this.

Eddie Cochran was a much bigger success in Britain than he was in the United States, where 'C'mon Everybody' only made No. 35 in the charts.[27] This may be because access to American rock 'n' roll was fairly limited in Britain, and because Cochran was one of the few musicians who toured the country. I think that the appeal in Britain of Cochran, and of Elvis and other rock 'n' roll singers, had a second dimension, apart from (but connected to) the music itself, namely their 'American-ness'. I have not yet read an account of that crucial cultural process which was the operation of the idea of 'America' in Britain in the 1950s.[28] No doubt this fantasy construct was partly the product of Hollywood movies, and of a variety of images of the economic, cultural and (as we had recently been grateful to discover) military power of the United States that were in circulation in Britain after the Second World War. Rock 'n' roll fed that fantasy. For some of us, I would say it *became* that fantasy. I have lost count of the number of my friends and colleagues from Britain, working in cultural studies, sociology, art history and film studies, who have ended up on the other side of the Atlantic in recent years. Mostly this emigration consists of refugees from Thatcherism, and of self-defined exiles from a collapsing system of higher education, which has long been under sustained and vicious attack. But I know from conversations with some of my co-deserters that this move, though motivated by political, educational and economic concerns, has often mobilized and realized that adolescent (and adult) dream of 'America'. The cultural history of the 1980s, which, amongst other things, will record the geographic shift of people and ideas, will also need to investigate the operation of the fantasy of 'America' in Britain in the 1950s, and its persistence and transformation since. Jean Baudrillard's book on America, composed as it is of the superficial and self-indulgent reflections and impressions of a European visitor, seems to me to be a missed opportunity to explore the meaning of 'America' in the post-war European consciousness.[29] For me, the irony of this aspect of the 'meaning' of Eddie Cochran was that by the time I did get to the United States, in 1969, they were playing the wrong music, and I found myself living in Philadelphia with friends recently returned from Woodstock, who spent the whole day playing music by James Taylor, Crosby, Stills and Nash, and – worst of all – the Beatles, who by then had just recorded *Abbey Road*.

Clearly, this is a personal account of the meaning of fifties music. For one thing, not everyone will agree with my view of Eddie Cochran as an important rock 'n' roll musician.[30] But my aim is not to correct the orthodoxy, to claim that the Beatles were *not* important, or to contest readings of Elvis different from my own. Nor, on the other hand, am I interested in simply offering some autobiographical reflections on my personal taste in music, or on the part specific musics have played in my life. I am working on the assumption that these preferences are not purely personal or idiosyncratic, but can be used to explore more general features of a cultural moment. Specifically, I want to address two related questions in this chapter. First, I am interested in the role of culture in the formation of identity: the ways in which we use certain cultural events, practices, objects in the continual process of our own production of self.[31] Secondly, I am interested in memoir as cultural history, and in using the personal and the subjective as access to social phenomena. In the next chapter, I discuss each of these, particularly the connection of the personal and the social, the concrete particular and the abstract general.[32] I consider some of the developments in critical theory which have led to this turn to the subjective and the specific in feminism and in cultural studies, particularly the critique of 'objectivity' (in philosophy and the social sciences, for example), dilemmas of ethnography (in anthropology and in popular culture studies), and the recognition of the need to interrupt the global narratives of social history and psychoanalysis from the point of view of those whose lives and experiences do not fit these accounts.[33] Here, I will not attempt to theorize about these issues, which are taken up more systematically elsewhere in this book. I am not even concerned to construct a coherent narrative across the three 'moments' which constitute this essay, or to make links between them. It will be clear, for instance, that my first episode (the Eddie Cochran moment) raises both the issue of culture and identity formation, and the issue of memoir as cultural history, as does my third (the Dark Sister), whereas the Donna Anna episode seems to have more to say about identity and less about social histories. I want to open up discussion of the intersections of the personal and the social, memory and cultural history, and the particular and the general.

The cultural theories at our disposal often simply do not work at the level of concrete experience. Social histories of class may, and may *have to*, ignore other significant issues (race, age, gender and so on). Feminist accounts of the family, modelled as they have usually been on the middle-class white family, have distorted and obscured the dynamics of working-class and black families. What is useful in these theories, however, can be retained in a critical engagement with them, which is located in the analysis of the particular. To begin with experience provides a different access to social histories (although, as I say in the following chapter, it also raises the complex question of the *typicality* of such experience, and of the extent to which we might generalize from it). The concept of 'experience' has come under suspicion since the advent of post-structuralism, being too quickly aligned with a suspect essentialism which posits the self and its experiences as an already constituted and centred entity. But I do not see that we need to succumb to essentialism or to pre-theoretical humanism in order to start from (or include) experience in cultural analysis. Indeed, it should be possible to demonstrate the constituted nature of experience in the process of its exploration. I would stress, then, that the model I am discussing, which moves from the abstractions of cultural theory to the experiential, is *not* one which substitutes the autobiographical narrative for theory. It is the *meeting point* of theory, social history and the particular (the 'micrological'). In relation to this development as, amongst other things, a response to the ethical and methodological dilemmas of ethnography, Katrina Irving has proposed the useful notion of an 'ethnography of the self' as a radically different, but perfectly respectable, way of doing cultural studies.[34]

My own attempts to work through particular cultural moments

and events are at this stage rather preliminary, and do not aspire to the intellectual and analytic rigour of, say, the 'dialectical image' (Benjamin) or the 'concrete particular' (Adorno), in which, through an immanent analysis of the object or phenomenon, the fundamental social structures and contradictions can be revealed. The moments originated not in theory (as illustrations of preformed ideas), but in memory, notebooks, therapy. It is only recently that I have been able to gain a greater understanding of the connection between my own experiences and cultural and feminist theory. (As a student in a graduate class in memoir writing at the University of Minnesota in 1989, I discovered that in a way I was unable to write straight-forward memoir, because my accounts were always processed through my immersion, over the years, in sociology and cultural studies. I saw this not as a failure to escape the deadening constraints of academic writing – constraints I have probably felt as long as I have been doing this work – or as the inevitable collapse of the 'creative' into the programmed, but rather as the potentially liberating pros-pect of that transformation of the academic which I had despaired of achieving.)

Like the Eddie Cochran moment, my second image has to do with music, but this time with opera. It takes me from April 1960 to an afternoon in November 1984, when I was driving between two Yorkshire towns and listening to a tape of Mozart's *Don Giovanni* on my cassette player.[35] This was a period in my life of disentangle-ment from a relationship, and at some level I was obviously working out issues of dependence and independence. Liz Heron, in her book of 'reflections on women's independence', explores the contradic-tions experienced by heterosexual women (herself and a variety of women she interviewed) in their relationships with men: desire for intimacy, fear of dependence, the pleasures and the loneliness of independence.[36] Psychoanalytic theory, too, has shown the origins (and explained the persistence) of these dilemmas for women,[37] and I was not short of intellectual tools when considering these issues. But Donna Anna was my short cut. I suddenly heard something I had never noticed before in the opera: the way Donna Anna (the only unseducible woman among Don Giovanni's victims,[38] the un-relentingly independent woman, avenging her father's murder) con-stantly surpasses the other singers in pitch and tone. When she sings 'Or sai chi l'onore' in her aria in Act 1, and when she interjects 'Io moro' and 'Resister non poss'io' in the finale of that act, her thrilling soprano voice overrides the complexities of sexual negotiation, resistance and seduction. Hers is the strong female voice, which seemed to me to express the possibilities of women's power. (Two years later, when I saw the opera performed, and perhaps when my circumstances were somewhat different, I had much more sympathy for Donna Elvira, the seduced woman who is still susceptible to the sexual and musical charm of the seducer. By then, Donna Anna seemed more of an inhuman aggressor, who had unfairly avoided women's dilemmas of dependence and independence by absconding altogether, and by changing the register of her song.[39])

Later I discuss the operation of gender ideologies in music, referring to Susan McClary's argument that in Bizet's *Carmen* the music itself requires Carmen's death, which coincides with the restoration of a dominant tonality and harmony and the silencing of her voice.[40] Here, as in my example of Donna Anna, the music works in conjunction with character and narrative to ensure the outcome, and, more importantly, to implicate the listener in desiring a particular resolution. In the same way, the songs of seduction in *Don Giovanni* achieve their effect, not just for the object of their address, but also for the audience, who *understand* the draw of the seducer whose very music insists on and secures assent – as when Don Giovanni sings to Zerlina 'Là ci darem la mano' and, in Act 2, to Donna Elvira's maid 'Deh vieni alla finestra'. So Donna Anna's high-pitched song of purpose, revenge and unassailability functions equally in an ideological and a musical register, speaking of women's power, and articulating for me the position of independence, strength and autonomy.[41]

Since my response to Donna Anna changed from one occasion to another, and from one performance to another, I am clearly not claiming any unvarying meaning of her voice for the listener. And, unlike the case of rock music, whose beat is 'corporeally invasive', I do not believe that the desires and emotions elicited by classical music (seduction, willing a death, whatever) are intrinsic to the music. On the contrary, they are the learned responses to culturally specific musical languages. What is the status, then, of my reading of Donna Anna? Its precariousness, my fickleness in relation to her character, precludes any attempt to identify her as a generic cultural text – the voice of an independent woman, for example – nor would I want to consider such a claim. My much more modest intention when citing that encounter with her voice is to illustrate the ways in which we use bits of culture in the incessant production of self. To the extent that such voices and figures operate more generally (that other people, too, engage with them in a similar enterprise), then personal memory would intersect again with cultural history; given the minority appeal of opera, however, and the particularly idiosyncratic nature of my one-time response, I do not wish to make any more of this case than to offer it as an example of cultural bricolage in the service of identity-work.

My third cultural image was crystallized in March 1988, at a performance in London's Royal Festival Hall of Tony Harrison's poetry-performance work, *Bow Down*.[42] Harrison is a social poet, born in Leeds and still based in the north of England. His work includes written poetry, plays, television drama-poems, opera libretti, and translations of verse texts from the original Greek and French. *Bow Down*, written in 1977, a collaboration with the composer Harrison Birtwistle, is a theatre work for actors and musicians. It tells the story of two sisters, in love with the same man. The man, who doesn't appear in the play, loves the younger more:

> He courted the eldest with jewels and rings
> But he loved the youngest best of all things . . .
> The eldest, she had a lover come,
> And he fell in love with the youngest one.[43]

The elder sister, reasonably enough, drowns the younger sister. The story of the drama tells what becomes of the drowned woman's body (a gruesome tale, involving horrendous fantasies of male violence), and includes the torture, confession and eventual death of the elder sister. I sat through this grisly narrative, until the last scene, in which the elder sister is being buried alive near the spot where her sister drowned. Then, already nauseated by the text and the drama, I suddenly found myself positioned as the unhappy murderess. The Chorus, calling for her death, chants

> Black your hair and black your soul,
> And black, . . . black, black the deep dark hole.[44]

And, indeed, throughout the play the sisters have been identified as the Fair Sister and the Dark Sister. In a note included in the published text of the play, Harrison says that 'the source material of *Bow*

Down was the ancient and traditional ballad of *The Two Sisters* which exists in numerous and varied versions throughout northern Britain, Scandinavia and America'.[45] At that moment, in a London concert hall, I realized that this opposition between fair and dark, good and evil, pervaded our culture and had played a crucial part in my own cultural formation. (This realization, new to me, is not, of course, new to critics who have explored the opposition in literary and other texts for some time.) The Fair Sister taunts the Dark Sister:

> Wash your hair in the salt sea brine
> it will never be as fair as mine
> Even if your hair was gold
> you'll always live alone and cold.
> Wash yourself as white as you can
> you will never find a man
> Wash yourself as white as bone
> but you'll always live alone.[46]

And the final Chorus sings:

> I'll make no strings of your dark hair,
> The tune would make the world despair.
> Lullabies with such black notes
> Choke cries of joy in children's throats.
> Ballads set to such dark lays,
> Make one night of all our days.[47]

Discussing the appeal of the natural and innocent sexuality of Marilyn Monroe, Richard Dyer emphasizes her blondeness, 'the ultimate sign of whiteness': 'The white woman is not only the most prized possession of white patriarchy, she is also part of the symbolism of sexuality itself. Christianity associates sin with darkness and sexuality, virtue with light and chastity.'[48] By the 1950s, the opposition was less extreme than it had been, 'but the associations of darkness with the drives model of sexuality and of fairness with female desirability remained strong'.[49] For me, this dominant cultural image was compounded by a marginalization as Jewish in a Christian culture. The negative construction of 'Jewishness' and 'darkness' relates to the primary opposition between black and white (which is not to say that being either Jewish or dark is *equivalent* to being black in white Western culture). Elsewhere, Dyer analyses the

filmic perception of black/white difference, where whiteness is associated with 'order, rationality, rigidity, qualities brought out by
contrast with black disorder, irrationality and looseness'.[50] And Sander
Gilman records the links made between Jews and blacks:

> The image of blackness projects much of the repressed anxiety sur-
> rounding the Jew's sexual identity in twentieth-century Europe. The
> depth of the association of the Jew with the black enabled non-Jewish
> Europeans during the nineteenth century to 'see' Jews as blacks. . . . The
> association of the images of 'blackness' and 'Jewishness' is a test case
> for the interrelationship of images of difference. The black and the
> Jew were associated not merely because they were both 'outsiders' but
> because qualities ascribed to one became the means of defining the
> difference of the other. The categories of 'black' and 'Jew' thus be-
> came interchangeable at one point in history.[51]

Klaus Theweleit, in the second volume of his monumental study of
the fantasies of members of the proto-fascist Freikorps in Germany
in the 1920s, finds that the Jewish woman is perceived as even more
dangerous, evil and threatening than the Jewish man.[52] Britain in the
1980s or 1950s is not Germany in the 1920s; and Jews are not
blacks. Nevertheless, there is clearly work to be done on the analysis
of Jewish difference in European culture, and on the intersections of
gender and Jewishness in that respect.

But there is more than ethnic difference in play in the fair/dark
opposition. Susan Bordo's work on representations of the female
body has shown the extent to which women's beauty is equated
with blondeness, pointing out, for example, advertisers' success in
promoting hair-straightening products and blue contact lenses (never
brown) for black women and dark women.[53] (The other side of
this pressure is seen in a recent case in which a white supremacist
shot and killed a plastic surgeon in Chicago and a hairdresser in
San Francisco on the grounds that they made their clients look more
Aryan by surgery and dyed hair, thus 'diluting the Aryan beauty'.
On his list for assassination, too, was a supplier of blue contact
lenses.[54]) From my point of view, the performance of Harrison's
work mobilized and articulated a life-long experience of exclusion
(though not one of discrimination or anti-Semitism) and, more
importantly, a certain partial self-identification as, somehow, 'bad'
(= dark).

There is not much of a connection between the three figures named in my title and explored in this chapter.[55] The three cultural moments and images I have described are at this stage nothing more than hints at how feminist cultural studies might connect the theoretical, the general and the experiential. One thing I am very aware of is the necessarily *eclectic* use of theory this kind of work engages in. Some of the debates in women's studies at the moment centre on this question of theoretical purity – particularly, I think, in film studies and in psychoanalytic theory.[56] Such purity can easily be sustained at the level of philosophical abstraction. It can probably also be more easily sustained in the analysis of texts, where, in a sense, it does not ultimately *matter* what interpretation one proposes. But cultural studies is not just about theories or texts: it deals with lived experiences, and with the intersections of social structures, systems of representation, and subjectivities – intersections which are, of course, relations of mutual constitution. Here it *does* matter if the interpretation does not fit experience.[57] (It is worth saying, however, that the kind of autobiographical or memoir-based work I have been discussing, primarily a middle-class and intellectual form of expression, is not the only access we have to the experiential. To this I would add the different traditions of working-class writing, the recording of oral histories, studies of reception, ethnography and psychoanalysis.)

Resistance to the distortions of theoretical orthodoxy both necessitates and justifies a more eclectic use of theory. The exploration of a cultural moment through the experiences of particular women's lives will not produce a single coherent narrative, but rather a series of distinct but overlapping perceptions. I do not take the postmodern view that we should abandon metanarratives, because I believe that there are certain crucial structures and tendencies in contemporary society, not just a fragmented, disconnected, anarchic set of phenomena, social relations and discourses. We still need theories of culture and society, in other words. But we also need *studies in* culture. From the point of view of feminism and cultural studies, this means employing a dual eclecticism: to use those theories that seem to work when exploring the cultural formation of identity, and to work with the bricolage of cultural events and moments through which the experience of culture is mediated and in which it is encapsulated.

NOTES

1 Of course, it wasn't really – this is poetic licence. There are plenty of other exceptions to my rather general history of the decline of rock after 1960. I could have added Creedence Clearwater to the Stones, for instance. I could have chosen, instead of Cochran's death, Elvis's induction into the army as the moment of the 'death' of rock 'n' roll.

2 *Rock of Ages, The Rolling Stone History of Rock & Roll* (Rolling Stone Press/Summit Books, 1986).

3 *Rolling Stone Rock Almanac* (Collier Books, 1983), p. 14.

4 *Rock of Ages*, p. 208.

5 *Rolling Stone Rock Almanac*, p. 86.

6 See, for example, Wilfrid Mellers, *Twilight of the Gods: The Beatles in Retrospect* (Faber and Faber, 1973).

7 Discussing the impact of Elvis in the 1950s, and the 'cover-up' of what he 'exposed' in subsequent years, Greil Marcus still comments, 'But what exactly it is that needs to be covered up remains as much a mystery as it ever was', *Dead Elvis: A Chronicle of a Cultural Obsession* (Doubleday, 1991), p. 124.

8 Paul Willis, *Profane Culture* (Routledge & Kegan Paul, 1978), p. 65.

9 Trent Hill, 'The enemy within: censorship in rock music in the 1950s', *South Atlantic Quarterly*, vol. 90, no. 4 (Fall 1991), special issue on *Rock & Roll and Culture*, edited by Anthony DeCurtis, p. 680.

10 Lawrence Grossberg, 'Is there rock after punk?', *Critical Studies in Mass Communication*, vol. 3 (1986), p. 52.

11 Allan Bloom's conservative critique of contemporary culture, *The Closing of the American Mind* (Simon & Schuster, 1987), is quite explicit about this: 'But rock music has one appeal only, a barbaric appeal, to sexual desire. . . . Young people know that rock has the beat of sexual intercourse. . . . In alliance with some real art and a lot of pseudo-art, an enormous industry cultivates the taste for the orgiastic state of feeling connected with sex.' (pp. 73–4)

12 David Buxton, 'Rock music, the star system, and the rise of consumerism', reprinted in Simon Frith and Andrew Goodwin (eds), *On Record: Rock, Pop, and the Written Word* (Pantheon Books, 1990), p. 432, originally published in *Telos*, no. 57 (1983).

13 See Andrew Chester, 'Second thoughts on a rock aesthetic: The Band', in *On Record*, p. 316 (first published in *New Left Review*, no. 67, 1970); Simon Frith: 'Towards an aesthetic of popular music', in Richard Leppert and Susan McClary (eds), *Music and Society: The Politics of Composition, Performance and Reception* (Cambridge University Press, 1987), p. 145.

14 Simon Frith, *Sound Effects: Youth, Leisure, and the Politics of Rock* (Constable, 1983), p. 165. The term 'grain of the voice' is taken from an essay by Roland Barthes. Marcus endorses the importance of the 'grain' of Elvis's voice: *Dead Elvis*, p. 38.

15 Interview in *New Musical Express*, 1958, quoted by Andrew Chester, in 'Second thoughts on a rock aesthetic', p. 316.

16 Where some writers unproblematically identify the roots of rock in black music, and that music in turn as African, others have been more careful to consider the constant historical mixing of 'black' and 'white' music. See Andrew Goodwin and Joe Gore, 'World Beat and the cultural imperialism debate', *Socialist Review*', vol. 20, no. 3 (1990), p. 71. Robert Pattison discusses the 'myth' of the history of music's progress from Africa via the Mississippi Delta to Elvis, and the idea of the 'primitive' which is in play in rock music, in *The Triumph of Vulgarity: Rock Music in the Mirror of Romanticism* (Oxford University Press, 1987), pp. 30–55.

17 Alan Sinfield, *Literature, Politics, and Culture in Postwar Britain* (University of California Press, 1989), p. 152. See also pp. 126–8, on black immigration into Britain in the 1950s.

18 Jon Savage, 'Sex, rock, and identity: the enemy within', in Simon Frith (ed.), *Facing the Music* (Pantheon Books, 1988), p. 150. This might be why, for example, Eddie Cochran was such a success in England.

19 David Shumway argues that we must think of rock 'n' roll not just as music, but as a 'historically specific cultural practice', involving many other aspects of behaviour and other objects (records, clothes, television and films): David R. Shumway, 'Rock & roll as a cultural practice', *South Atlantic Quarterly*, vol. 90, no. 4 (Fall 1991). Simon Frith examines the role of the music in answering questions of identity on the part of listeners, who are 'placed' in relation to social groups: Frith, 'Towards an aesthetic of popular music', pp. 140–4. Lawrence Grossberg, in similar terms, understands the investment in particular musics as a process of defining identity, using what he calls 'mattering maps': Grossberg, 'Is there a fan in the house? The affective sensibility of fandom', in Lisa A. Lewis (ed.), *The Adoring Audience: Fan Culture and Popular Media* (Routledge, 1992).

20 See Simon Frith and Angela McRobbie, 'Rock and sexuality', reprinted in Frith and Goodwin (eds) *On Record*, originally published in *Screen Education*, no. 29 (1978).

21 Sue Wise, 'Sexing Elvis', reprinted in Frith and Goodwin, *On Record*. Originally published in *Women's Studies International Forum*, vol. 7 (1984).

22 See John Clarke, Stuart Hall, Tony Jefferson and Brian Roberts, 'Subcultures, cultures and class', in *Resistance through Rituals: Youth*

Subcultures in Post-war Britain (Hutchinson, 1976), originally published as *Working Papers in Cultural Studies* 7 and 8 (Summer 1975) (Centre for Contemporary Cultural Studies, University of Birmingham).

23 'Dance Criticism: Feminism, Theory and Choreography', where I oppose the notion of the immediacy of the body, and the assumption that dance is pre-social or 'natural'.

24 There is support for this in John Miller Chernoff's discussion of the integral relationship of music and dance in Africa: *African Rhythm and African Sensibility* (University of Chicago Press, 1979), pp. 143–51.

25 Cochran/Capeheart, Liberty Records (1958).

26 Dave Marsh, *The Heart of Rock & Soul: The 1,001 Greatest Singles Ever Made* (New American Library, 1989), p. 235. Other assessments of him include the following: 'Cochran's virile tenor was the key element in the success of [the] songs, but he is best known for the primitive intensity of his guitar playing', in H. Wiley Hitchcock and Stanley Sadie (eds), *The New Grove Dictionary of American Music*, vol. 1 (Macmillan, 1986), p. 461; 'Along with Chuck Berry and Buddy Holly, he was one of the great singer/songwriters of rock and roll – a chronicler of teenage rebellion, excitement, and frustration . . . His vocal style . . . was near to Elvis Presley's, moody and rough', in Peter Gammond: *Oxford Companion to Popular Music* (Oxford University Press, 1991), p. 122; 'Perhaps the finest exponent of teenage rockabilly, Cochran wrote and recorded one of the classic adolescent anthems, "Summertime Blues". His early death cut short the career of a major guitar stylist, as well as a potentially great rock songwriter', in Phil Hardy and Dave Laing, *The Faber Companion to 20th-Century Popular Music* (Faber and Faber, 1990), p. 153.

27 *The Rolling Stone Encyclopedia of Rock & Roll* (Rolling Stone/Summit Books, 1983), p. 109.

28 But Dick Hebdige has written about the horrified reaction of the British establishment to what it perceived as the Americanization of culture – youth cultures, rock 'n' roll, 'juke box boys' and milk bars: 'Towards a cartography of taste 1935–1962', in *Hiding in the Light* (Comedia/Routledge, 1988). I attempt to address this question of 'America' in Britain in a later essay in this book: 'Angry Young Men and Minor (Female) Characters'.

29 Jean Baudrillard, *America* (Verso, 1988).

30 Marsh describes Cochran as 'the most overrated fifties rocker . . . an average singer and prolific, able songwriter': *The Heart of Rock and Soul*, pp. 524–5.

31 See Frith, 'Towards an aesthetic of popular music'; Grossberg, 'Is there a fan in the house?' See also the essays in Alan Tomlinson (ed.),

Consumption, Identity, & Style: Marketing, Meanings, and the Pack-aging of Pleasure (Comedia/Routledge, 1990).

32 'Memoirs and Micrologies, Walter Benjamin, Feminism and Cultural Analysis'.

33 Carolyn Steedman's book, *Landscape for a Good Woman* (Virago, 1986) seems to me a wonderful model of this kind of intervention.

34 This was in a response to both this paper and one by Lee Quinby, at a conference at SUNY Binghamton in March 1990. Quinby's paper has since been published as 'The subject of memoirs: *The Woman Warrior*'s technology of ideographic selfhood', in Sidonie Smith and Julia Watson (eds), *De/colonizing the Subject: The Politics of Gender in Women's Autobiography* (University of Minnesota Press, 1992).

35 The recording was of Joseph Losey's film of the opera (CBS Inc., 1979), Donna Anna is sung by Edda Moser.

36 Liz Heron, *Changes of Heart: Reflections on Women's Independence* (Pandora, 1986).

37 See, for example, Christiane Olivier, *Jocasta's Children: The Imprint of the Mother* (Routledge, 1989).

38 This is contested. See, for example, Julian Rushton, *W. A. Mozart, Don Giovanni* (Cambridge University Press, 1981), p. 59, and the fictional account by Sylvia Townsend Warner, *After the Death of Don Juan* (Virago, 1989 [1938]).

39 Then, too, it might have been the different performance, the different performer and the different voice that produced new meanings.

40 'Death and the Maiden, Does Semiotics Justify Murder?'

41 See Ralph P. Locke, 'What are these women doing in opera?', *Opera News*, August 1992.

42 Tony Harrison, *Bow Down*, 1977, in *Theatre Works 1973–1985* (Penguin, 1986).

43 Ibid., p. 129.

44 Ibid., p. 147.

45 Ibid., p. 126.

46 Ibid., p. 132.

47 Ibid., p. 148.

48 Richard Dyer, *Heavenly Bodies: Film Stars and Society* (Macmillan, 1987), pp. 43, 44.

49 Ibid., p. 44.

50 Richard Dyer, 'White', *Screen* vol. 29, no. 4 (Autumn 1988), pp. 47–8.

51 Sander L. Gilman, *Difference and Pathology: Stereotypes of Sexuality, Race, and Madness* (Cornell University Press, 1985), pp. 34–5. See also his 'The Jewish nose. Are Jews white?, or the history of the nose job', in *The Jew's Body* (Routledge, 1991).

52   Klaus Theweleit, *Male Fantasies*, vol. 2, *Male Bodies: Psychoanalyzing the White Terror* (University of Minnesota Press, 1989), p. 13.

53   Susan Bordo, '"Material girl": the effacements of postmodern culture', *Michigan Quarterly Review*, vol. XXIX, no. 4 (Fall 1990), special issue on *The Female Body* (Part 1). See also Teresa Podlesney, 'Blondes', in Arthur and Marilouise Kroker (eds), *The Hysterical Male: New Feminist Theory* (St Martin's Press, 1991).

54   *New York Times*, 11 August 1993.

55   Mike Groden has suggested to me that a connecting theme is death: the death of Eddie Cochran, the death of a relationship, the death of the Fair and Dark Sisters. It is an intriguing suggestion, though I am not sure quite what to do with it in this context.

56   See, for example, Constance Penley, 'Introduction. The lady doesn't vanish: feminism and film theory', in *Feminism and Film Theory* (Routledge/BFI, 1988); Toril Moi, 'Patriarchal thought and the drive for knowledge', in Teresa Brennan (ed.), *Between Feminism and Psychoanalysis* (Routledge, 1989).

57   This is one of the premises of Steedman's project, in *Landscape for a Good Woman*.

3

Memoirs and Micrologies: Walter Benjamin, Feminism and Cultural Analysis

This chapter is not about getting Walter Benjamin 'right'. I want to resist the more radical post-structuralist and hermeneutic readings of his work that are in evidence these days, in which a 'reader's' Benjamin is preferred to a 'historicized "historical" and "political" Benjamin', as the editor of one collection of essays has put it;[1] but I have also come to the conclusion that there is not much profit in entering the debates, fifty years old and still going strong, about a *correct* interpretation of Benjamin's position. It is not that I think these debates are unimportant: I do believe it has been essential to consider the question of the contradiction, resolution, or perhaps sequential development of Benjamin's theological and materialist modes of analysis and whether, for instance, 1924 constitutes an epistemological break. In fact some of my argument will depend on taking a position on these issues.

But having now immersed myself for some time in the contemporary versions of the Scholem/Brecht/Adorno claims on Benjamin, re-staged by (respectively) George Steiner/Terry Eagleton/Rolf Tiedemann and Susan Buck-Morss, and diplomatically mediated by Julian Roberts, Richard Wolin and Michael Jennings, I want to suggest that an examination of the contemporary appropriations of Benjamin's work is more interesting. Although 'getting Benjamin right' continues to be important for Benjamin-scholarship, and for the historical record, it is not necessary or even relevant from the point of view

of what is being done now, in the late twentieth century, in his name
and on the basis of what people *think* he said. Of course, misinter-
pretations, as much as interpretations, can tell us something about
the political and intellectual projects in play in such appropriations,
but here I want to look at the appropriations themselves. Specifically, I am interested in the current revival of interest in Benjamin's
work in cultural criticism and cultural studies. My focus is on work
in the Anglo-American traditions, and my particular concern is feminist cultural studies. I will make a few suggestions about the basis
of the appeal of Benjamin for this work – the points of special
congruence between his essays and some current concerns. And I
will try to justify my own reservations about this romance. I think
there are real problems, and certain risks, involved in the whole-
hearted enthusiasm for Benjamin (or 'Benjamin') that we are wit-
nessing in contemporary cultural criticism, and I will address these
later.

In case any justification were needed for the selective and motivated reading of the text, it is of course already there in Benjamin
himself, as two of his main English-language commentators have
pointed out. Michael Jennings concludes that

> when we use Benjamin to a particular end or in the service of a
> particular cause . . . we are always proceeding in a Benjaminian way,
> not so much in that we use his ideas to construct our own critical
> constellations but in that we 'mortify' Benjamin's own words, we rip
> them from their context and so expose Walter Benjamin's own pre-
> tensions to a higher knowledge.[2]

Susan Buck-Morss, for the same reasons, argues that 'in the service
of truth, Benjamin's own text must be "ripped out of context",
sometimes, indeed, with a "seemingly brutal grasp".'[3] Two of
Benjamin's clearest statements about historical method and the dialectical image (a notion, as I will suggest, which is not unproblematic),
both in Konvolut N of the Arcades Project, insist on this:

> It isn't that the past casts its light on the present or the present casts
> its light on the past: rather, an image is that in which the Then (*das
> Gewesene*) and the Now (*das Jetzt*) come into a constellation like a
> flash of lightning. In other words: image is dialectics at a standstill.
> (N 2a, 3)

> The destructive or critical impetus in materialist historiography comes into place in that blasting apart of historical continuity which allows the historical object to constitute itself . . . Materialist historiography does not choose its objects casually. It does not pluck them from the process of history, but rather blasts them out of it. (N 10a, 1)[4]

I do not read this as licence for distortion, or for the free play of ungrounded readings: the insistence that objects are not chosen casually, I think, takes care of that. Before I consider Benjamin and cultural criticism, then, I want to discuss why I resist certain contemporary readings of Benjamin's work, as I am also arguing against textual orthodoxy.

In the introduction to his 1981 book on Benjamin, Terry Eagleton states his intention to write about Benjamin 'in order . . . to get at him before the opposition does'.[5] The opposition is the literary–critical establishment, the effect of whose efforts is to depoliticize Benjamin's project. More recently, Michael Jennings has suggested the national or geographical basis for disparate appropriations, according to which 'American readers have tended . . . to stress Benjamin as a close reader, and to glorify, through Romantic tropes, Benjamin the brooding genius', ignoring the philosophical emphasis of his work in favour of the literary.[6] I share the critical point of view of these remarks, but am no longer sure it is possible to argue for them in any absolute terms. For one thing, as half a century of Benjamin-criticism has made clear, the work is so notoriously elusive and, often, contradictory that it is really impossible to deny alternative readings. More importantly, however, as Benjamin himself argued and as more recent work on historiography and metahistory has demonstrated, historical accounts are always in some sense interpretations, and competing analytical or sociological models cannot, ultimately, ever be shown to be fundamentally 'right'. This is something that is at issue currently with regard to the translation of cultural studies to the United States. Commentators like Cary Nelson and John Clarke have argued convincingly that the original project of cultural studies (at least in its Birmingham mode) has been transformed and depoliticized in the trans-Atlantic shift.[7] Cultural studies in the United States is now both a growth industry and a high-profile approach, as a recent special issue of the *Village Voice Literary Supplement*, devoted to the subject, confirms.[8] But in its new incarnation in the Modern Language Association, cultural studies has become simply a new way of reading texts, in which any social–historical perspective itself becomes textualized (with new-historicist and post-structuralist justifications for the move), and in which the political meanings and effects of texts have little to do with the institutional and social structures of their production and reception, or with ethnography and actual readers or viewers. Yet I think we have to be wary of claiming 'the truth' for cultural studies, on the basis of authenticity, historical accuracy, or biographical authority (e.g. 'I was at Birmingham myself'). Here I agree with Stuart Hall; positioned, despite himself, as the primary speaker at the block-buster Cultural Studies conference in Champaign-Urbana two years ago, he refused the implicit invitation to put everyone right:

> I don't want to talk about British cultural studies . . . in a patriarchal way, as the keeper of the conscience of cultural studies, hoping to police you back into line with what it really was if only you knew. . . . I'm going to tell you about my own take on certain theo-retical legacies and moments in cultural studies, not because it is the truth or the only way of telling the history.[9]

Therefore, and for similar reasons, all I want to say here about a particular, North American reading of Benjamin, which for conven-ience I label the 'Johns Hopkins version', is that I really have no interest in it. (This is, of course, not to say that we could not also examine its location, its politics, and its implications, but that it is not necessary or, in the end, possible to prove it 'wrong'.)

As Gershom Scholem once said, Benjamin's prose manifests an 'enormous suitability for canonization'.[10] It seems that this cente-nary year is already the occasion for new activities of this kind,[11] though we will have to wait to see what residues the various con-ferences and conference volumes will have after 1992. With regard to cultural criticism and cultural studies the revival of interest in Benjamin's work in worth examining, because the reasons and inter-ests behind this are no longer what they were in earlier enthusiasms. In German studies, Benjamin scholarship has proceeded uninter-rupted; in Britain and, especially, in the United States, there have been new translations, and secondary texts, and discussions in *New German Critique* and other journals. But the involvements of cul-tural theory have been spasmodic and more than a little selective. In the early and mid-1970s there were two main versions of 'Benjamin' in circulation, identified centrally with the essays 'The author as producer' and 'The work of art in the age of mechanical reproduction'.[12] The particular sets of interest here were, first, that represented in *New Left Review* (and New Left Books) and *Screen* – an interest in questions of cultural politics, which focused on Benjamin's relationship with Brecht and read 'The author as producer' in that context; and second, an interest in media technology and specifically the implications of reproducibility, hence in photography, film and media studies. The second of these, particularly, is still an important debate, with the proliferation of new technologies, especially in relation to pop music (sampling, questions of copyright and so on), but also other media, for example the recent copyright case involving visual artist Jeff Koons. The 'work of art' essay continues to be reprinted in anthologies,[13] and Benjamin is often the starting point for discussing contemporary modes of cultural reception and participation.[14] But, as Julian Roberts pointed out in the early 1980s, interest in Benjamin seemed to wane after the mid-1970s. Ironically, this occurred at a time when more of his work was becoming available: notably the 'Notes and Materials' of the *Arcades Project* in 1982 (in German), and (in English) the essays in *One-Way Street* and *Reflections*, 'Konvolut N', 'Central Park' and the *Moscow Diary*.[15] So the secondary books of the 1980s (Roberts, Eagleton, Smith and others) did not really engage with an active critical culture focused on his work. For a while, interest in Benjamin in cultural criticism was confined to the study of modernity.[16] Cultural studies for the most part was still preoccupied with Gramsci and Foucault, grappling with post-structuralism and post-modern theory, and being transformed by feminism and post-colonial criticism (and with regard to these last two, despite some recent claims, Benjamin is not a great help).

There are two important reasons for the current revival of interest in Benjamin's work in cultural studies: memoirs and micrologies. That is, the interplay of the autobiographical and the critical in his work accords well with contemporary tendencies to integrate these two modes of writing; at the same time, the analytics of the concrete are very much in tune with the current rejection of abstract theory and the desire for specificity. The rest of this chapter will consider the appeal and the risks of each of these strategies. It has occurred to me, however, that there are other reasons for that 'canonization' of which Scholem speaks; they probably merit examination, but I will simply identify and discuss them briefly here. Four that come to mind are: The Photograph; The Tragedy; The Exile; The City.

It has always seemed remarkable to me how much those *photographs* figure in Benjamin's texts. More than with any other author I can think of, it has seemed almost obligatory to include at least one image on the cover, the frontispiece or in the body of the text. Susan Sontag's essay on Benjamin begins with a discussion of some of the best-known photographs, as if the way to read the texts is through the life, itself read through the icon: indeed, she proceeds to do just that.[17] Despite all we know about the mediation of the image (thanks, partly, to Benjamin's own work), we are constantly implicated in some fantasy of immediate knowledge of the author, compounded by the way in which most interpretations do situate the text in relation to the biography. There is a potentially interesting project here, in the analysis of the circulation and production of meaning of these images of the author.

They relate, too, to the *tragedy* of the life, and here I am thinking of what we know about other cultural heroes. There is no doubt that tragedy, and particularly suicide, 'fixes' and defines a life (and, hence, the work) in specific ways. In popular culture, the figures of Marilyn Monroe, James Dean and Jim Morrison – their myths, filmic and other biographical inventions, and canonization in the posters and T-shirts of youth culture – are only the most obvious of many examples. In the history of art, critics have demonstrated the ways in which the work of Van Gogh and Mark Rothko has been interpreted through the suicide of those artists, which is seen to define the life (which will inevitably lead to suicide and which is, hence, tragic all along); the life, thus constructed, in turn determines the readings of the visual texts.[18] (Early or accidental death works nearly as well as suicide in this respect, for example in the cases of Jackson Pollock and Jack Kerouac.) We have not yet had the biopic of Benjamin's life (though we have had at least one novel based on his last years[19]), but I do think there is a possible study to be made of the operation of this late twentieth-century phenomenon in relation to Benjamin's appeal.

The glorification of *exile* works in a similar, though more complex, way. (Sontag's essay is relevant here, too, with its themes of melancholy, solitude, the Saturnian personality.) Here I would say there are a number of different things going on. First, the romanticization of Benjamin which Jennings identifies in contemporary literary studies is greatly assisted by the notion of Benjamin as the 'outsider' – as, indeed, have been all romantic notions of the artist since the nineteenth century. His constant geographical mobility and his final seven years of exile are merely convenient physical expressions of that outsider status, which is also manifest, for example, in his marginality to the academy, to intellectual schools of thought and to the family. There is also a new romanticism of exile in play today, which has to do with the politics of post-coloniality. Nobody, of course, wants to be identified with the centre, with that oppressive, dominant, static position, and the result has partly been the proliferation of claims to alterity.[20] For those who do not claim outsider status – a politics of exile – the new ethnography provides the possibility of non-dominating, dialogic knowledge.[21] Although the more radical accounts of this project can seem somewhat disingenuous in their disavowal of power relations by simple methodological devices, the insistence on self-reflexivity as a minimal requirement is a valuable, if less ambitious, development (with a respectable pedigree in critical theory).

In addition, however, the *intrinsic* value of the outsider status is less clear. Julian Roberts at one point suggests that being a full professor at Frankfurt University necessarily inhibited the political aspect of the work of the director of the Institute for Social Research, and that Benjamin's association with the Institute produced for him the same risks of compromise.[22] And in an essay in the most recent issue of *Cultural Studies*, Angela McRobbie, arguing the importance of Walter Benjamin for contemporary cultural studies, gives as one of her central reasons his status as an academic outsider.[23] But this can only be another kind of romanticization, on a level with the Photo and the Tragedy. At the very least, it needs to be shown (sociologically and epistemologically) why marginality produced better insights. Karl Mannheim had a theory about this (the free-floating intelligentsia), but there are equally good theories of knowledge that argue the opposite case and identify, as Foucault does, the specific intellectual or, as Gramsci does, the organic intellectual – both of these structurally and ideologically related to, even *central* to, social groups.[24]

Lastly, I would say that the current interest in Benjamin's work has a lot to do with his *city* portraits:[25] the essays on Naples, Marseilles, Moscow and Berlin, as well as the major work on Paris. The city is at the moment an important focus of analysis, across a range of disciplines: urban sociology, political economy, urban geography, art history. Theories of urban space are much debated, particularly with the recent translation of work by de Certeau and Lefebvre.[26] I am not entirely sure how the *city* and *exile* are related. On the one hand Peter Szondi claims that Benjamin wrote no more city portraits after 1933 because exile makes it impossible – as he puts it 'with the loss of one's homeland the notion of distance also disappears. If everything is foreign, then that tension between distance and near-ness from which the city portraits draw their life cannot exist. The emigrant's . . . map has no focal point'.[27] Benjamin himself, on the other hand, makes the somewhat cryptic note (in 'Central Park'): 'Emigration as a key to the metropolis'.[28] In any case, here I simply record the convergence of certain contemporary concerns with a central aspect of Benjamin's oeuvre.

Commentaries on Walter Benjamin have consistently discussed his writings in relation to his life. This is not only true of Gershom Scholem's biographical memoir, but also of the essays by Susan Sontag, Hannah Arendt and George Steiner which introduce three volumes of Benjamin's texts.[29] Even Adorno's intellectual portrait of Benjamin begins with the sentence 'The name of the philosopher who took his life while fleeing Hitler's executioners has, in the more than twenty years since then, acquired a certain nimbus, despite the esoteric character of his early writings and the fragmentary nature of his later ones'.[30] But of course Benjamin's own work operates on the borderline of subjective experience, memory and cultural analy-sis. There are the straightforwardly autobiographical texts (notably 'A Berlin chronicle' and *A Berlin Childhood around 1900*[31]); the personal, memoiristic essays ('Hashish in Marseilles'[32]); the individ-ualistic and subjective city portraits (of Moscow, Marseilles and Naples[33]); and the diary extracts (*Moscow Diary*, 'Conversations with Brecht'[34]), not intended for publication. Even in the philosophical and literary critical texts we are often confronted with the personal moment – as, for example, in the essay on 'Surrealism' when Benjamin recalls his hotel in Moscow in which Tibetan lamas always left their doors ajar.[35] I believe this interplay between the analytic and the subjective-personal is an important factor in the current interest in returning to Benjamin. In particular there are three areas in cultural criticism where memoir is being taken seriously at the moment: feminist literary theory, cultural history and popular culture studies.

Women's autobiographical writing has recently become highly visible. I mean this not just in the sense that more autobiographies are being published (which is probably true), or even that there has been a proliferation of essays of autobiographical reflection by women writers (which is also the case),[36] but rather that feminist literary critics are directly addressing the question of the *nature* of women's autobiographical writing, and the ways in which women construct the 'self' through writing – what Domna Stanton calls 'autogyno-graphy'.[37] The post-structuralist critique of the existential subject has opened up the possibility, indeed the necessity, of exploring the discursive processes through which identities are produced and maintained. Feminism has a particular investment in this, in line with the now well-known rejoinder to charges of essentialism and identity politics; as Nancy Miller has put it, 'the postmodern deci-sion that the Author is dead, and subjective agency along with him, does not necessarily work for women and prematurely forecloses the question of identity for them. . . . women have not . . . felt burdened by too much Self, Ego, Cogito.'[38] The emphasis here is on the pol-itical importance of identity, combined with the analytic realization that identity is always provisional. In addition, feminist literary critics, including Miller, have been arguing the need to integrate the per-sonal *into* academic work – what Miller refers to as 'getting per-sonal' and Mary Ann Caws as 'personal criticism'.[39] This is partly to do with being explicit and self-reflexive about one's engagement with the subject-matter; so one way to consider this move is as con-tinuing the feminist project of the denial of 'objectivity' and distance, construed as 'masculine' and already challenged in philosophy by Susan Bordo and in the philosophy of science by Evelyn Fox Keller[40]. But it is also about a more clearly political choice, about the decision to identify and select certain texts and situations as worth studying, and about the willingness to state the basis of one's commitment to them.

In cultural studies and cultural history, too, the transformation of method (and hence of histories themselves) by the autobiographical interruption has been radical. I am thinking here of Carolyn Steed-man's book, *Landscape for a Good Woman*,[41] in which she inter-rogates the stories constructed by social historians, feminists and psychoanalytic critics from the vantage-point of real lives: her own and her mother's. The inadequacies, gaps and distortions in such overarching theories become apparent in the oblique gaze made pos-sible by the memoir. Steedman's experiment is explicitly motivated by political as well as personal passion and has already provided the model for others who want to resist the tyranny of grand theories, the threat of excessively deconstructed identity, and the professional requirements of depersonalized academic writing. Essays in cultural studies and cultural analysis now routinely include the author in the text.

For quite different reasons, this has happened too in popular culture studies, where analysts have recently been preoccupied with their own relationships to their subjects. Janice Radway has reflected on the nature of her involvement with the readers of popular fiction, about whom she wrote in her book *Reading the Romance*.[42] Constance Penley felt she needed to wonder aloud and in print about her relationship to the pornographic Star Trek literature and its fans, the subject of her recent research, to the extent of examining just how much she responded to the literature herself.[43] Here the issue is the ethical one of resisting any relationship of exploitation; in this it shares with the 'new anthropology' a commitment to re-think ethnographic method as a dialogic process. One result of this concern has been the incorporation of fragments of memoir, diary and other modes of self-reflection in the text.

All of these are important developments in cultural theory. I believe it is essential to transform ethnographic method and to deconstruct or at least acknowledge power relations in sociological research, and that writing is a crucial arena for the production and articulation of identity. And I am also interested in breaking down the boundaries between academic and personal writing; my own work is increasingly, though tentatively, at the meeting point of cultural theory, gender studies and memoir. So my reservations about certain formulations of this project (and hence of the new enthusiasm for Benjamin's work, which I believe is related to these) have to do with how we may proceed with and what we may expect from such strategies. For one thing, as I indicated earlier in relation to the 'new ethnography', I contest the view that power relations between researcher and subject evaporate if we just manage to be dialogical enough in our research methods; it is still a matter of an encounter motivated, set up and more or less controlled by one party, whatever the sensitivity and 'openness' to the other. Secondly, self-reflection need not be politically radical, ethically correct or analytically illuminating. It *can* be simply self-indulgent, embarrassing and irrelevant. And thirdly, it cannot be simply assumed that the memoiristic provides guaranteed access to knowledge, because we still have to address the question of typicality.

So where the personal is valuable in laying bare the structures and prejudices of cultural work, it does not necessarily provide the route to better cultural history, unless we can be persuaded that this particular experience is somehow *typical* or indicative of a moment.

These comments relate, too, to the last thing I want to address, namely the equivocal appeal of micrological analysis in cultural studies. Here it is not only Benjamin who is in vogue today. Although, of course, these operate in the context of very different discourses and theoretical projects, I would link the Benjaminian concepts of the *monad*, the *dialectical image* and the *constellation* to Barthes' notion of the *punctum*, Bakhtin's concept of the *chronotope*, Derrida's concept of the *trace* and Adorno's discussion, influenced by Benjamin, of the *concrete particular*,[44] all of which have been taken up recently in cultural criticism. It is clear that there is a real attraction to 'micrological' approaches (as both Bloch and Adorno have described Benjamin's method[45]). I think this is partly a reaction to a growing dissatisfaction with the abstractions of Theory. To some extent, too, it is related to the desire for the connection with the personal and the subjective, which I have been discussing. Naomi Schor has made a specifically feminist case for 'the detail', as historically associated with the 'feminine' and for that reason worth studying;[46] and Norman Bryson, in his recent book on still-life painting, associates the downgrading of this genre, with its very specific attention to detail, with its identification with feminine space and women's art practice.[47] And both semiotic and psychoanalytic approaches to cultural analysis lend themselves to a focus on the concrete detail. As I said with regard to the memoir, I do not intend to question either the desire to work with the micrological or the various factors which have prompted it. I believe that, at its best, micrological analysis can be enormously productive for a broader social and cultural history. But I am worried, too, about the risks.

Concerns about thinking in images have informed a good deal of the debate about Benjamin's legacy. Michael Jennings puts it carefully when he says that 'Benjamin's construction of constellations of images is not risk free'.[48] Buck-Morss and Richard Wolin have both drawn a distinction between Benjamin's more materialist grounding of the dialectical image and his 'intuitive', quasi-mystical accounts, which verge on the irrational.[49] Behind this lies the classic debate with Adorno, according to whom Benjamin's unmediated use of the concrete is quite unacceptable. I do not see that there is much to be gained from joining the discussions on how Marxist Benjamin was (though I will say that I have not been persuaded by those who argue that his invocation of commodity fetishism, which seems to me to be more arbitrary than structural and systematic, rescues his project from theology and redeems it for materialism). But whether or not the dialectical image (or the monad – an earlier version of the significant concrete detail) is firmly grounded in historical material-ism, I do want to maintain that it has to be grounded in *something*. In principle, it is very likely that certain constellations capture for us the dynamic and the contradictions of a historical moment or a cultural event, and often do so by by-passing the contortions and pedantries of theory (though, of course, they are never purely naive or primitive; they are never innocent of theory). I worry about the invisible exclusions which always come into play with the adoption of such micrologies, and therefore want to conclude my comments on Benjamin's appeal by considering this from the point of view of feminist cultural studies.

What counts as a dialectical image? Even in Benjamin's writing, this is far from clear, partly because his general discussions of the image (in Konvolut N and the Surrealism essay, for example, or the discussion of the monad in the Prologue to *Trauerspiel* study) do not connect with the micrological thinking elsewhere. So, for instance, it seems that some of the titles of the 36 Konvoluts do identify dialectical images in relation to nineteenth-century Paris[50] – the ar-cades, fashion, the interior, the *flâneur*, the prostitute – while others ('the theory of knowledge') do not. What is the basis of their selec-tion? In an essay on 'the invisible *flâneuse*', I have argued that the identification of the figure of the *flâneur* as a central figure of modernity, epitomizing the urban experience (an idea we find not only in Baudelaire and Benjamin but also in Simmel and later writ-ers like Marshall Berman and Richard Sennett), totally excludes women.[51] This means that 'modernity' is defined entirely from the point of view of men, since women were not (and, for that matter, are not) at liberty to engage in aimless and anonymous strolling. The equation of 'modernity' with the public arena has important im-plications for gender studies. This is not because the public sphere was male and the private sphere female: as many feminist historians have pointed out, women – particularly working-class women – have always had access to the public. Rather, the *ideology* of appro-priate spaces operates to deny the connection of public with female, and to pathologize or marginalize women who *are* in evidence in the street. My point here, then, is that a central dialectical image carries with it crucial gender connotations, none of which are acknowledged or thought through. Recently, certain feminist re-readings of Benjamin have been proposed. Rey Chow suggests that the aimless, non-purposive character of strolling and loitering is a 'feminine' mode and, further, that there is good evidence of Benjamin's rejection of the mother and alliance with the prostitute.[52] Victor Burgin has argued that we should understand the arcades as a maternal space, representing the pre-Oedipal moment.[53] I am not sure how to assess these proposals, but I still want to insist that thinking in images comes with risks, and that Benjamin's images collude with a patriarchal construction of modernity.

Is the *collector* (another Konvolut category) an example of a dialectical image? If so, it can be shown that this is similarly gendered. Schor, in her article on postcards of Paris in 1900, has argued that the collector, or rather the basis for the desire to collect, may be primarily male.[54] Clearly for Benjamin the *interior* is a central image, and one, we might think, that balances the masculine focus on the street on which the image of the *flâneur* depends. However, like Adorno in his discussion of the bourgeois interior in the study of Kierkegaard,[55] Benjamin has nothing to say about the gender dimensions of the interior space.[56] Rather, the bourgeois woman is rendered invisible in his discussion of the interior as the counterpart of the office[57] and as the habitat of the collector, who moulds the traces of his living in the interior.[58] And where the micrological focus *is* on a woman, as in the case of the prostitute, as Buck-Morss has pointed out, the whore is reduced to a sign.[59] In 'Central Park', Benjamin makes the perceptive but cryptic remark that 'Baudelaire never once wrote a whore-poem from the perspective of the whore'.[60] But for Benjamin too the prostitute stands for a male-defined set of possibilities and sexual and economic meanings.

I am not trying to take Benjamin to task for a lack of prescience of feminist scholarship of the past twenty years; but I do want to stress that, as a product of his time, his work has certain limitations, and that in the case of 'thinking in images' we have to be especially alert to how these operate, because their 'immediate' character will not necessarily direct us to their theoretical orientation. This applies to all attempts to short-cut theory with images, tropes, chronotopes or metaphors. In another chapter I argue this in relation to the current proliferation of metaphors of *travel* in cultural theory.[61] Like Adorno, I am asking for a theory of mediations, or at least for a willingness on the part of micrological thinkers to explore the origins and connotations of the images which figure in their analyses. My hope is that it will then prove possible to learn from Benjamin, and to revive and transform a deadening and depersonalized academic discourse with memoirs and micrologies.

NOTES

1 Rainer Nagele, 'Introduction: Reading Benjamin', in *Benjamin's Ground: New Readings of Walter Benjamin* (Wayne State University Press, 1988), p. 9.
2 Michael W. Jennings, *Dialectical Images: Walter Benjamin's Theory of Literary Criticism* (Cornell University Press, 1987), p. 213.
3 Susan Buck-Morss, *The Dialectics of Seeing: Walter Benjamin and the Arcades Project* (MIT Press, 1989), p. 340. The quotations are from 'Konvolut N'.
4 Walter Benjamin, 'N [Re the theory of knowledge, theory of progress]', in Gary Smith (ed.), *Benjamin: Philosophy, History, Aesthetics* (University of Chicago Press, 1989, first published in *The Philosophical Forum*, vol. 15, nos 1–2, 1983–4), pp. 50 and 66.
5 Terry Eagleton, *Walter Benjamin, or Towards a Revolutionary Criticism* (Verso, 1981), p. xii.
6 Jennings, *Dialectical Images*, p. 4.
7 Cary Nelson, 'Always already cultural studies: two conferences and a manifesto', *Journal of the Midwest Modern Language Association*, vol. 24, no. 1 (1991); John Clarke, 'Cultural studies: a British inheritance', in *New Times and Old Enemies: Essays on Cultural Studies and America* (Harper Collins, 1991); Mike Budd, Robert M. Entman and Clay Steinman: 'The affirmative character of US cultural studies', *Critical Studies in Mass Communication*, vol. 7 (June 1990); Graham Murdock, 'Cultural studies: missing links', *Critical Studies in Mass Communication* (December 1989).
8 *Village Voice Literary Supplement* (April 1992).
9 Stuart Hall, 'Cultural studies and its theoretical legacies', in Lawrence Grossberg, Cary Nelson and Paula Treichler (eds), *Cultural Studies* (Routledge, 1992), p. 277.
10 Gershom Scholem, 'Walter Benjamin and his angel', in Gary Smith (ed.), *On Walter Benjamin: Critical Essays and Recollections* (MIT Press, 1988), p. 51. Buck-Morss also uses this term, referring to

Benjamin's 'brilliant writing, which we are so predisposed to canonize': *The Dialectics of Seeing*, p. x.

11 This paper was originally presented at a conference celebrating the centenary of Benjamin's birth, at Birkbeck College, London, July 1992.

12 These were published in English in *Understanding Brecht* (New Left Books, 1973) and *Illuminations* (Harcourt, Brace & World, 1968). 'The author as producer' is also included in *Reflections* (Harcourt Brace Jovanovich, 1978) and in Andrew Arato and Eike Gebhardt (eds), *The Essential Frankfurt School Reader* (Urizen Books, 1978).

13 For example, John G. Hanhardt (ed.), *Video Culture: A Critical Investigation* (Visual Studies Workshop Press, 1986).

14 For example, John Mowitt, 'The sound of music in the era of its electronic reproducibility', in Richard Leppert and Susan McClary (eds), *Music and Society: The Politics of Composition, Performance and Reception* (Cambridge University Press, 1987); Andrew Goodwin, 'Sample and hold: pop music in the digital age of reproduction', *Critical Quarterly*, vol. 30, no. 3 (1988).

15 *One-Way Street and Other Writings* (New Left Books, 1979); *Reflections: Essays, Aphorisms, Autobiographical Writings* (Harcourt Brace Jovanovich, 1978); 'N [Re the theory of knowledge, theory of progress]', in Smith (ed.), *Benjamin*; 'Central Park', *New German Critique*, no. 34 (Winter 1985).

16 For example, David Frisby's study, *Fragments of Modernity: Theories of Modernity in the Work of Simmel, Kracauer and Benjamin* (Polity Press, 1985), and some essays in the journal *Theory, Culture & Society*.

17 Susan Sontag, 'Under the sign of Saturn', in *A Susan Sontag Reader* (Farrar, Straus and Giroux, 1982).

18 On Van Gogh, see Griselda Pollock, 'Artists, mythologies and media: genius, madness and art history', *Screen*, vol. 21, no. 3 (1980), as well as John Berger's discussion of 'Wheatfield with Crows', in *Ways of Seeing* (Penguin, 1972), pp. 27–8. On Rothko, see J. R. R. Christie and Fred Orton, 'Writing on a text of the life', *Art History* vol. 11, no. 4 (1988).

19 Elaine Feinstein, *The Border* (Hutchinson, 1984).

20 See, for example, Gayatri Spivak, 'Who claims alterity?', in Barbara Kruger and Phil Mariani (eds), *Remaking History* (Bay Press, 1989); Edward Said, 'The politics of knowledge', *Raritan*, vol. xi, no. 1 (1991).

21 James Clifford and George E. Marcus (eds), *Writing Culture: The Poetics and Politics of Ethnography* (University of California Press, 1986); George E. Marcus and Michael M. J. Fischer, *Anthropology as Cultural Critique: An Experimental Moment in the Human Sciences* (University of Chicago Press, 1986).

22   Julian Roberts, *Walter Benjamin* (Macmillan, 1982), p. 66.
23   Angela McRobbie, 'The *Passagenwerk* and the place of Walter Benjamin in cultural studies: Benjamin, cultural studies, Marxist theories of art', *Cultural Studies*, vol. 6, no. 2 (May 1992).
24   I discuss the question of knowledge and social location in chapter 1.
25   See Peter Szondi, 'Walter Benjamin's city portraits' (1962), in Smith (ed.), *On Walter Benjamin*.
26   Michel de Certeau, 'Walking in the city', in *The Practice of Everyday Life* (University of California Press, 1984); Henri Lefebvre: *The Production of Space* (Basil Blackwell, 1991 [1974]). See also Derek Gregory and John Urry (eds), *Social Relations and Spatial Structures* (Macmillan, 1985); *Strategies*, vol. 3, 1990: special issue, 'In The City'; *New Formations*, no. 11 (1990), 'Subjects in Space'.
27   Szondi, 'Walter Benjamin's city portraits', p. 31.
28   Benjamin, 'Central Park', p. 42.
29   Gershom Scholem, *Walter Benjamin. The Story of a Friendship* (Schocken Books, 1981); Susan Sontag, 'Under the sign of Saturn' (Introduction to *One-Way Street*); Hannah Arendt, 'Walter Benjamin: 1892–1940', Introduction to *Illuminations* (Jonathan Cape, 1970, originally published as an article in the *New Yorker*); George Steiner, Introduction to Walter Benjamin's *The Origin of German Tragic Drama* (New Left Books, 1977).
30   Theodor W. Adorno, 'A portrait of Walter Benjamin', in *Prisms* (Neville Spearman, 1967), p. 229.
31   'A Berlin chronicle' is in *Reflections* and *One-Way Street*. Part of *A Berlin Childhood around 1900* appears in English in *Art and Literature: An International Review*, no. 4 (1965) (Lausanne).
32   In *Reflections* (first published 1932).
33   All reprinted in *Reflections*; 'Moscow' originally in 1927; 'Marseilles' in 1929; 'Naples' in 1925.
34   *Moscow Diary* (Harvard University Press, 1986); 'Conversations with Brecht' in *Understanding Brecht*.
35   In *Reflections*, p. 180.
36   For example, Carolyn Anthony (ed.), *Family Portraits: Remembrances by Twenty Distinguished Writers* (Doubleday, 1989); Janet Sternburg (ed.), *The Writer on her Work* (W. W. Norton, 1980).
37   Domna C. Stanton, 'Autogynography: is the subject different?', in *The Female Autograph: Theory and Practice of Autobiography from the Tenth to the Twentieth Century* (University of Chicago Press, 1987). See also: Estelle C. Jelinek (ed.), *Women's Autobiography: Essays in Criticism* (Indiana University Press, 1980); Carolyn G. Heilbrun, *Writing a Woman's Life* (W. W. Norton, 1988); Shari Benstock (ed.), *The Private Self: Theory and Practice of Women's Autobiographical Writings*

(University of North Carolina Press, 1988); Bella Brodzki and Celeste Schenck (eds), *Life/Lines: Theorizing Women's Autobiography* (Cornell University Press, 1988); Sidonie Smith, *A Poetics of Women's Autobiography* (Indiana University Press, 1987).

38 Nancy Miller, 'Changing the subject: authorship, writing, and the reader', in Teresa de Lauretis (ed.), *Feminist Studies/Critical Studies* (Indiana University Press, 1986), p. 106.

39 Nancy K. Miller, *Getting Personal: Feminist Occasions and Other Autobiographical Acts* (Routledge, 1991), especially the essay 'Getting personal: autobiography as cultural criticism'; Mary Ann Caws, 'Personal criticism: a matter of choice', ch. 1 of *Women of Bloomsbury* (Routledge, 1990).

40 Susan Bordo, 'The Cartesian masculinization of thought', *Signs* vol. 11, no. 3 (1986); Evelyn Fox Keller: *Reflections on Gender and Science* (Yale University Press, 1985).

41 Published by Virago, 1986.

42 *Reading the Romance: Women, Patriarchy and Popular Literature* (University of North Carolina Press, 1984). See also her comments at a conference on Cultural Studies: pp. 78–9 of Lawrence Grossberg, Cary Nelson and Paula Treichler (eds), *Cultural Studies* (Routledge, 1992); and her essay 'Reception study: ethnography and the problems of dispersed audiences and nomadic subjects', *Cultural Studies*, vol. 2, no. 3 (1988).

43 Constance Penley: 'Feminism, psychoanalysis, and the study of popular culture', in Grossberg, Nelson and Treichler (eds), *Cultural Studies*, p. 484. She asks, 'Where did I fit in to all this? – was I going to the conference as a fan, even perhaps a potential writer of K/S stories, a voyeur of a fascinating subculture, or a feminist academic and critic?' She concludes that it was all three.

44 See Susan Buck-Morss, *The Origin of Negative Dialectics* (Harvester Press, 1977) pp. 69–76.

45 Ernst Bloch, 'Recollections of Walter Benjamin', in Smith (ed.), *On Walter Benjamin*, p. 340; Adorno, 'A portrait of Walter Benjamin', p. 236.

46 Naomi Schor, *Reading in Detail: Aesthetics and the Feminine* (Methuen, 1987).

47 Norman Bryson, *Looking at the Overlooked: Four Essays on Still Life Painting* (Harvard University Press, 1990), ch. 4, 'Still life and "feminine" space'.

48 Jennings, *Dialectical Images*, p. 32.

49 Buck-Morss, *Dialectics of Seeing*, p. 220; Richard Wolin, *Walter Benjamin: An Aesthetic of Redemption* (Columbia University Press, 1982), pp. 179–81.

50   Here I am following scattered references in Susan Buck-Morss's book, the major study of the dialectical image to date, for example pp. 176 (interior), 185 (prostitute), 211 (commodity), 221 (arcades, exposition, fashion).

51   'The invisible *flâneuse*: women and the literature of modernity', *Theory, Culture & Society*, vol. 2, no. 3, 1985: reprinted in *Feminine Sentences: Essays on Women and Culture* (Polity/University of California Press, 1990). See also 'The Artist and the *Flâneur*' in this volume.

52   Rey Chow, 'Walter Benjamin's love affair with death', *New German Critique*, no. 48 (1989).

53   Victor Burgin, 'The city in pieces', *New Formations*, no. 20 (1993). See also Elizabeth Wilson's essay, 'The invisible *flâneur*', *New Left Review*, no. 191 (1992), which, like her book *The Sphinx in the City* (Virago, 1991), reclaims the city for women, for example suggesting that the prostitute is the *flâneuse* of the nineteenth century city (p. 105).

54   Naomi Schor, '*Cartes postales*: representing Paris 1900', *Critical Inquiry*, vol. 18 (Winter 1992), pp. 201–2.

55   Theodor W. Adorno, *Kierkegaard: Construction of the Aesthetic* (University of Minnesota Press, 1989), pp. 40–6.

56   For example, 'Louis-Philippe or the Interior', in 'Paris – the capital of the nineteenth century', *Charles Baudelaire: A Lyric Poet in the Era of High Capitalism* (New Left Books, 1973).

57   'The private citizen who in the office took reality into account, required of the interior that it should support him in his illusions.' Ibid., p. 167.

58   Ibid., p. 169.

59   Susan Buck-Morss, 'The *flâneur*, the sandwichman and the whore: the politics of loitering', *New German Critique*, no. 39 (1986), p. 122.

60   Benjamin, 'Central Park', p. 42.

61   'On the Road Again: Metaphors of Travel in Cultural Criticism'.

4

Death and the Maiden: Does Semiotics Justify Murder?

I recently watched a video of Woody Allen's *Crimes and Misdemeanors*. I had seen the film twice before, and was trying to remember exactly how Schubert figured in the story. What I recalled was that Dolores Paley (the character played by Anjelica Huston) mentions Schubert, in an irritatingly girlish moment with her lover, Judah Rosenthal (Martin Landau); later, as she walks back to her apartment at night, and to her death (arranged by Judah under pressure of her blackmail), the soundtrack plays the slow movement, the 'death' theme, of Schubert's D minor Quartet, 'Death and the Maiden'. My memory was of the musical coding of her death, in a sequence which rendered it as inevitable as the logic of Judah's agonized decision.

I was partly right. She does ask Judah to teach her about Schubert (although she confuses him with Schumann, until Judah puts her right – Schumann is 'flowery', but Schubert, who reminds him of her, is 'the sad one'). In another scene she threatens to come to the family house and expose their affair unless he meets her right away at a nearby gas station. When he turns up, in pouring rain, they sit in the car and she gives him a small package (it is his birthday) saying she knows how he loves Schubert. Shortly after this, Judah is finally persuaded that he has to let his brother, with his criminal connections, eliminate her. As she walks home, stopping at a liquor store for a bottle of wine, the Schubert plays in the soundtrack. It is the first non-diegetic music in the film.

However, it turned out to be not the D minor Quartet (No. 14, D 810), but the slow movement of Quartet No. 15 in G major (D

887). The movement *is* in a minor key (E minor), confirming Judah's description of Schubert as 'sad', and the music certainly operates to produce an atmosphere of anxiety and premonition. According to John Reed, the Quartet manifests a 'tone of melancholy nostalgia'.[1] But it is the D minor Quartet, as Reed also says, that is about death.[2] So unless I conclude that *this* Schubert metonymically stands for 'Death and the Maiden' (by association, or by proximity, being the next-composed quartet), I am at a loss to understand the 'meaning' of 'Schubert' in the filmic text, a text in which meanings are carefully, and often explicitly, produced for the viewer – for example in the film's recurring metaphor of eyes/seeing.

Why does it matter? I am interested in how narratives, including musical ones, insist on women's deaths. Elisabeth Bronfen's brilliant study *Over Her Dead Body* explores the intersections of death, femininity and the aesthetic with regard to literary and visual texts, in a semiotic/psychoanalytic framework; it demonstrates a certain necessary connection, in representation and in the psychic economy, between Woman and Death.[3] Both femininity and death, she argues, 'cause a disorder to stability, mark moments of ambivalence, disruption or duplicity and their eradication produces a recuperation of order, a return to stability' (p. xii). Through a lengthy, sometimes difficult, but always lucid examination of textual themes and tropes – dead brides, hysterical women, speaking corpses, wax models, the portrait, the dead beloved as muse – she demonstrates the psychic and representational mechanisms through which a patriarchal culture defines alterity and sustains the illusion of identity. Fear of the feminine (and this fear she explains in various ways, for example as the fear of re-engulfment in the mother) and fear of death are ultimately fear of loss of control and of the disruption of boundaries between self and Other (p. 182) – of a return to symbiotic unity and de-differentiation.

The originality of Bronfen's book lies in its refusal to participate in that kind of feminist criticism which identifies and indicts the murderous patriarchal text. Two important quotations recur in the book, one by Edgar Allan Poe, the other by Walter Benjamin. Poe's notorious statement that 'the death of a beautiful woman is, unquestionably, the most poetical topic in the world',[4] appears on the back of Bronfen's book (in fact in a rather misleading way, because it seems to promise that other kind of feminist critical reading which Bronfen rejects). The statement is addressed directly by her in chapter

4, where she resists the obvious interpretation of nineteenth-century misogyny, instead accepting the *truth* of Poe's assertion and analysing the cultural connections between beauty, femininity and death. As Bronfen puts it,

> It is crucial ... that the production of beautiful images (aesthetics) and the construction of femininity are culturally equated because they are analogously positioned in relation to death. The beauty of Woman and the beauty of the image both give the illusion of intactness and unity, cover the insupportable signs of lack, deficiency, transiency and promise their spectactors the impossible – an obliteration of death's ubiquitious 'castrative' threat to the subject.[5]

The quotation from Benjamin equates creativity with the death of the feminine:

> One has often thought of the creation of great works of art in the image of birth. This image is dialectical; it circumscribes the process in two directions. One has to do with creative conception ... and its genius concerns femininity. This femininity exhausts itself after the ful- filment. ... It gives life to the art work and then dies. ... In the pro- cess of being fulfilled the creation gives birth once again to the creator. Not in his feminine mode, in which his creation was conceived, but rather in his masculine element.[6]

Again, Bronfen's project is not to take Benjamin to task for an unthinking sexism in his view of creativity, but instead to take ser- iously his recognition of the cultural associations of masculine cre- ativity and feminine death in which we are all necessarily implicated by virtue of the particular regime of representation and psychic structures we inhabit.

The difference between semiotics and ideology-critique is very clear here. There is no question, for instance, of explaining these gender meanings in relation to structures of power and the ideologies which sustain them. We learn from Bronfen, and from any sensitive semiotic/ psychoanalytic account, that in an important way it is beside the point to object to such instances of patriarchal damage – and here, to their most extreme form, the death and sometimes murder of women. It is beside the point because these formulations are not simply the reflections of a patriarchal or misogynist culture, much less the incitement to or justification of such acts. Instead, they state and re-state the meaning of the feminine in our culture, and the task is to begin by decoding them. This is very different from a feminist ideology-critique whose intention is to expose such texts, and in some cases to outlaw them. In arguing the importance of Bronfen's project, however, I do not intend to counterpose a crudely censoring and undertheorized feminism to a more subtle and sophisticated one. Nor is this in anything but the simplest terms a replay of those debates on pornography, in which we have come to see a polarization – real or imagined – between radical feminist pro-censorship and psychoanalytic theoretical feminist toleration and appreciation. On the contrary, I want to consider what is lost, politically and analytically, in the abandonment of ideology-critique. For although I do not really believe that understanding amounts to collusion, there is a way in which the semiotic/psychoanalytic approach seems to evacuate the arena of feminist contestation. But do we not still want to object that the death or murder of women (and the poetical idealization of this) is not such a good idea? I am not raising the difficult question of the 'real' here – that continuing confrontation between certain post-structuralist textualizing moves on the one hand, and unreconstructed sociological positions on the other – particularly as Bronfen's own project is quite specifically about texts. (I will come back to this issue later.) The point, then, is not to move from issues of representation to the horrors of actual violence against women. But I do think there is an important issue, to do with the circulation of these women/death tropes in our culture. Another thing that concerns me, to which I will return later, is the constant ability of semiotics to discover the subversive moment in the oppressive text. To do so may be essential for this approach if it is not to collapse into total pessimism in the face of the inherent and pervasive gender-coding in contemporary culture, but the risk (as we have also seen in recent work in the study of popular culture) is the excessive belief in limitless and ubiquitous opportunities for revolt and challenge, discovered in the most unlikely cultural texts and institutions.

I come back to music (not discussed by Bronfen) to address these two issues. Susan McClary has suggested that the death of Carmen is determined not only by the narrative of the story (the Mérimée original and Bizet's opera), but also, importantly, by the music.[7] Carmen's song refuses to be contained by the tonal and harmonic requirements of nineteenth-century music. McClary claims that Carmen's music is grounded in the body, the rhythms of her song making this clear. In addition, 'Carmen's music is further marked by its chromatic excesses',[8] for example in the 'Habañera'. In the end, the audience is implicated in desiring Carmen's death (the silencing of her song) by the rules and expectations of conventional musical language. As McClary puts it elsewhere, 'It is [Carmen's] harmonic promiscuity – which threatens to undermine Don Jose's drive for absolute tonal closure at the conclusion of the opera – that finally renders her death *musically* necessary'.[9]

Although McClary makes it clear that her aim is not to indict this work and others like it for their 'monstrous feminine images or deadly narrative strategies',[10] she is not interested in the deeper analysis of the psychic-representational structures that produce such gender images. She concludes with a hope for 'new models of gender and desire: models that do not pit mind against body, that do not demand shame – or death – as the price for sexual pleasure.'[11] In this she stands somewhere between Bronfen, who might point out that such models are inconceivable, and the kind of ideology-critique that *would* indict *Carmen* for its sexism and look for more acceptable narratives.

I take this example for a number of reasons. In the first place, McClary's work and that of other feminist musicologists show that the same narrative and ideological strategies of gender are at work in musical, literary, visual and filmic texts. Secondly, the tone and passion of McClary's writing retrieves that sense of outrage at the normalization of the death of women that characterized 1970s feminist literary criticism and its straightforward hostility to the misogynistic text; in McClary's case, however, it is with the advantage of a less simplistic understanding of the relations between representation, ideology, and social relations.[12] Perhaps we cannot have it both ways; since, as Bronfen shows, the death of women is both intrinsic and 'necessary' to our cultural and psychic identity, in one sense it is not a matter for aesthetic or political critique and legislation. Yet I want to leave room, too, for ideology-critique, for a feminism that can still operate at the level of exposing the connections between misogyny, representation and the structural relations of power and inequality with regard to gender.

My third reason brings me back to the question of alternatives and resistances. McClary acknowledges that even though Carmen has to die, her voice persists. 'We leave the theatre humming her infections tunes, and the closure that had seemed so indisputable opens up again'.[13] Bronfen identifies possibilities for women writers, who are able to work through the topos of woman/death and its aporias in a simultaneous complicity and contestation.[14] Her examples are Sylvia Plath, Fay Weldon, Margaret Atwood and Angela Carter, all of whom 'install the cultural paradigm that links femininity with death in the same gesture that they critique it'.[15] Here, at least, is some relief from a prospect of relentless and total immersion in a cultural economy which needs to link women and death. But this raises the problem of contrary readings. Can we not read *any* text to find an alternative voice?

It would be interesting to identify an equivalent example of a contestatory *visual* text. On the cover of Bronfen's book is reproduced Henry Fuseli's *The Nightmare,* in which an incubus sits on the body of an unconscious young woman (plate 1). (Freud had a reproduction of this work in his study.) The painting is not discussed in her text, and perhaps this is not surprising, though I imagine Bronfen had some say in its choice for the cover. For this is not an image of a *dead* woman, but of a *sleeping* one. And it recalled for me, in this context, a 1983 painting by the feminist artist Alexis Hunter entitled *A Struggle between Ambition and Desire*, in which a catlike creature of the night also sits on a sleeping woman (plate 2). As soon as I picked up Bronfen's book I was, because of this association, already thinking about the power of the sleeping woman, who will soon awaken.

Let me conclude by returning to 'Death and the Maiden'. Schubert's Quartet in D minor, which is 'about death', takes for its central (death) movement the theme of one of his songs, written a few years earlier in 1817. The song, also entitled 'Death and the Maiden', is based on a poem of Matthias Claudius, again of the same title, published in 1775. The poem and the song consist of two stanzas, the first spoken by the Maiden (who attempts to resist Death), the second by Death (who persuades and seduces). Death, then, has the last word. But it has proved possible to interpret this exchange as incomplete, because the Maiden's own words can be seen as seductive ('geh, Lieber' – 'go, dear one') and because 'the poem ends before the moment of death occurs'.[16] Of course, if the composer is concerned about the last word, he can easily repeat the first stanza in the musical setting; Brahms, in using Hölderlin's 'Hyperions Schicksalslied' as the text for his own 'Schicksalslied', was so concerned

1 Henry Fuseli, *The Nightmare*, 1781, oil on canvas, 102 × 127 cms. The Detroit Institute of Arts. Gift of Mr and Mrs Bert L. Smokler and Mr and Mrs Lawrence A. Fleischman.

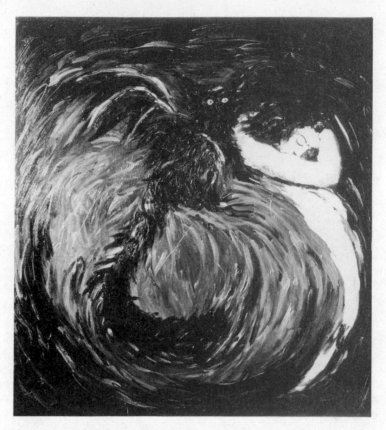

2   Alexis Hunter, *A Struggle between Ambition and Desire*, 1983, oil
on canvas, 14 × 15 cms. Private collection, London. © Alexis
Hunter, 1995.

that the first two blissful stanzas were followed and negated by a
final pessimistic verse, that he had the orchestra repeat the earlier,
euphoric themes to close the piece.[17] But then, as with Carmen, can
we still say we are left with the memory of the provisionally silenced
voice of despair? There must be a limit to this kind of hermeneutic
optimism; at least we must be clear that when we identify subversive
moments in the text we are talking about potential reading practices
rather than textual possibilities. Otherwise the two main and pecu-
liarly contradictory problems with semiotics are these: first, that our
immersion in a dominant and oppressive regime of representation is
total; second, that there is always the possibility of oppositional

textual strategies. Often this amounts to identifying the same text as both conservative and liberatory. The dual solution to this kind of meaninglessness is a semiotics grounded in ideology-critique (that is relating textual meanings to structures and ideologies of inequality) and an ethnographic understanding of reading practices (in opposition to ingenious textual interpretation). It is clear to me, at least, that the Maiden does die, even if we can sometimes listen to her voice against the grain of the text.

NOTES

1 John Reed, *Schubert* (J. M. Dent & Sons, 1987), p. 154.
2 Ibid., p. 153.
3 Elisabeth Bronfen, *Over Her Dead Body: Death, Femininity and the Aesthetic* (Manchester University Press, 1992).
4 This occurs in his essay, 'The Philosophy of Composition', quoted by Bronfen on p. 59 of her book, and referred to throughout it.
5 Bronfen, *Over Her Dead Body*, p. 64.
6 Walter Benjamin, *Denkbilder*, quoted by Bronfen, pp. 124–5.
7 Susan McClary argues this in three places: in her Foreword to Catherine Clément's *Opera, or the Undoing of Women* (University of Minnesota Press, 1988); in 'Sexual politics in classical music', in her *Feminine Endings: Music, Gender, and Sexuality* (University of Minnesota Press, 1991); in her *Georges Bizet: Carmen* (Cambridge University Press, 1992).
8 McClary, 'Sexual politics in classical music', p. 57.
9 McClary, Foreword to Clément, *Opera*, p. xiii.
10 McClary, 'Sexual politics in classical music', p. 79.
11 Ibid., p. 79.
12 McClary's work has been criticized for a tendency towards essentialism and universalism, as well as for oversimplifying musical issues – for instance for a lack of recognition of the prevalence of chromaticism in other nineteenth-century music. For example, David Schiff, 'The bounds of music', *The New Republic*, 3 February 1992; Ruth A. Solie, 'What do feminists want? A reply to Pieter van den Toorn', *The Journal of Musicology*, vol. IX, no. 4 (Fall 1991); Mary Ann Smart, review forthcoming in *Journal of Musicological Research*.
13 McClary, *Georges Bizet: Carmen*, p. 110.
14 Bronfen, *Over Her Dead Body*, p. 406
15 Ibid., p. 432.
16 Herbert Rowland, *Matthias Claudius* (Twayne, 1983), pp. 109, 110.
17 William Mann, Notes to EMI recording (27 0313 5), 1985.

5

Dance Criticism: Feminism, Theory and Choreography

The climactic moment in Brian Friel's play *Dancing at Lughnasa* comes half-way through the first act, when the five Mundy sisters break into a wild spontaneous dance around their kitchen. The sisters, aged twenty-six to forty, live two miles outside the village of Ballybeg in County Donegal, Ireland. The oldest, Kate, is a teacher; two of the others make some money by knitting gloves. The play, set in 1936, is a narrative of hopelessness, apparently based to some extent on the playwright's reminiscences of his own aunts;[1] its only moments of redemption and transcendence are brief and have to do with music and dance. The persistent focus of the play is the wireless set (named 'Marconi' by the sisters, 'because that was the name emblazoned on the set'[2]), which works only intermittently. The dance is inspired by Irish dance music which the wireless plays after a new battery is connected. The stage directions make it clear that this is a transgressive moment: 'With this too loud music, this pounding beat, this shouting-calling-singing, this parodic reel, there is a sense of order being consciously subverted, of the women consciously and crudely caricaturing themselves, indeed of near-hysteria being induced.'[3] The music stops, and after a while the dancers stop, somewhat embarrassed and ashamed, but also defiant. There are two other moments of dance in the play, one when Chris, the youngest sister, dances in the garden with Gerry, the father of her illegitimate son, the other when Gerry dances with another sister, Aggie, also in the garden of the cottage. Mostly the play is about *not* dancing, and in particular about the fact that the sisters never do get to the dance at the harvest festival of Lughnasa, despite an early passionate expression of desire to do so. The narrator (Chris's son, now a man) concludes the play by relating the drab and tragic future of these sisters and then returns to the memory of dance at 'that Lughnasa time':

> When I remember it, I think of it as dancing. Dancing with eyes half closed because to open them would break the spell. Dancing as if language had surrendered to movement – as if this ritual, this wordless ceremony, was now the way to speak, to whisper private and sacred things, to be in touch with some otherness. Dancing as if the very heart of life and all its hopes might be found in those assuaging notes and those hushed rhythms and in those silent and hypnotic movements. Dancing as if language no longer existed because words were no longer necessary.[4]

Here I think dance operates both as a literal idea and as a metaphor. It is literal because there is in our contemporary culture a notion that to dance is to be free. It is also metaphorical, because of course dancing in itself would not have liberated these women from the social and economic hardships: dance, rather, stands for the possibility of escape. I suspect that the surprising success of this play, which was nominated for eight Tony awards and won three and which was retained for many weeks at the Plymouth Theatre in New York,[5] has to do with its moments of transcendence in a terminally depressing narrative (not the kind that will usually captivate a theatre or cinema audience in the United States) and with its confirmation of the liberating power of dance. But why do we think of dance as liberating? It seems to me that there is a strong but for the most part unexamined belief in the equation dance=freedom, which dates particularly from the advent of modernism (that is the late nineteenth century) and which is evident in a wide variety of literary and other texts. This equation operates especially in relation to gender.[6] It is women's dancing, more than men's, that symbolizes their desired or imminent social liberation.

More recently, this dance metaphor has migrated into cultural criticism (and particularly feminist criticism).[7] In this chapter I explore the uses of the dance metaphor in theory, and make some suggestions about the reasons for such 'dance criticism' and its appeal for feminism. I believe that the adoption of vocabularies of dance and choreography is based on a misunderstanding of the nature of dance. Perhaps ironically, this has been made possible by the precritical state of dance studies. As the academic study of dance begins to take account of work in cultural studies, critical theory (including post-structuralist theories) and the sociology and social history of the body, we are in a better position to understand the semiotic and social meaning of the dance.[8] Dancing may well be liberating, and the metaphor of dance may sometimes capture the sense of circumventing dominant modes of rationality. But my concern about this particular trope is that it depends on a mistaken idea of dance as intuitive, non-verbal, natural, and that it risks abandoning critical analysis for a vague and ill-conceived 'politics of the body'.

The Mundy sisters are not the first women to dance inappropriately. Nora's tarantella in Ibsen's *A Doll's House* is an earlier example.[9] Her final departure from her marriage is prefigured by the wildness of her dance, as she rehearses for her performance. 'Slower, slower!' says Helmer, 'Not so violently, Nora. . . . No, no, this won't do at all', and then 'But, Nora darling, you're dancing as if your life depended on it. . . . You've forgotten everything I taught you.'[10] Although she is temporarily brought back into line, in the end she does escape from her claustrophobic domestic existence. Jane Marcus has suggested that Nora's dance parallels Salome's ('her only art form'), for each of them the sole means of expression.[11] In both cases, too, it is clear that the dancing woman is presented as a threat to patriarchy or at least to particular men; this is more obvious in the case of Salome, whose dance is the direct cause of the death of John the Baptist, his head her reward for dancing before Herod. Marcus's essay focuses on Oscar Wilde's version of Salome, which she perceives as unusually sympathetic to women, to 'the revolutionary potential of female desire'.[12] (This attitude she sees sustained in Richard Strauss's operatic setting of the play. She contrasts it, however, with Beardsley's illustrations for Wilde's play and with other representations, notably those by Moreau and Huysmans, which portray Salome negatively, as perverse and decadent.) For both Nora and Salome, the dance and its consequences signify the transgression of social roles.

The case of Salome is interesting inasmuch as the dance itself, so central to our contemporary reading of the story, is relatively unimportant in earlier versions. The biblical sources of the story simply tell us the following: 'But when Herod's birthday was kept, the daughter of Herodias danced before them, and pleased Herod. Whereupon he promised with an oath to give her whatsoever she would ask.' (Matthew 14:6–7.) 'And when the daughter of . . . Herodias came in, and danced, and pleased Herod and them that sat with him, the king said unto the damsel, Ask of me whatsoever thou wilt, and I will give *it* thee.' (Mark 6:22.) Salome is not named in these texts; nor is the dance described.[13] In Wilde's version,[14] the stage directions are minimal, the description of the dance absent: 'Salome dances the dance of the seven veils.'[15] In Strauss's opera, too, there are only brief stage directions, but the 'Dance of the Seven Veils' is orchestrated; indeed, years later Strauss wrote a detailed descriptive treatment of the dance itself, in relation to the music.[16] So in the performative versions of the text (play and opera) there is dramatic space for the dance, which therefore figures importantly in the narrative. Unlike the biblical texts, these modern versions necessarily foreground the moment of dance, as textual brevity cannot be translated into an equivalent insignificance on stage: either Salome dances or she doesn't.

It is not accidental that the dance and hence the story of Salome take on a certain importance at the moment of modernism in the arts. A crucial text is Joris-Karl Huysmans's lengthy discussion of Salome in his novel *A Rebours* (*Against Nature*). His Salome is in fact the figure depicted by the painter Gustave Moreau in 1876 (plate 3). Huysmans's description of the painting manifests a horrified fascination with the sensual female body:

> With a withdrawn, solemn, almost august expression on her face, she begins the lascivious dance which is to rouse the aged Herod's dormant senses; her breasts rise and fall, the nipples hardening at the touch of her whirling necklaces; the strings of diamonds glitter against her moist flesh; her bracelets, her belts, her rings all spit out fiery sparks; and across her triumphal robe, sewn with pearls, patterned with silver, spangled with gold, the jewelled cuirass, of which every chain is a precious stone, seems to be ablaze with little snakes of fire, swarming over the mat flesh, over the tea-rose skin like gorgeous insects with dazzling shards, mottled with carmine, spotted with pale yellow, speckled with steel blue, striped with peacock green.[17]

For Des Esseintes, the novel's protagonist, Moreau's Salome represents his most decadent desires:

> She had become, as it were, the symbolic incarnation of undying Lust, the Goddess of immortal Hysteria, the accursed Beauty exalted above all other beauties by the catalepsy that hardens her flesh and steels her

3 Gustave Moreau, *Salome dancing before Herod*, 1876, oil on canvas, 143.5 × 104.3 cms. The Armand Hammer Collection, The Armand Hammer Museum of Art and Cultural Center, Los Angeles, California.

muscles, the monstrous Beast, indifferent, irresponsible, insensible, poisoning, like the Helen of ancient myth, everything that approaches her, everything that sees her, everything that she touches.[18]

Of course, a painting can only portray a static moment in the dance, and in fact Huysmans's account similarly freezes the movement rather than recording the dancer's steps. But the story of Salome here clearly focuses on the dance, for Moreau as for Huysmans.[19]

4   Gino Severini, *Dancer with Moveable Parts*, 1915, oil on canvas,
60 × 49 cms. Fondazione Magnami-Rocca, Parma. © ADAGP,
Paris and DACS, London, 1995.

For visual artists in the period of early modernism the dance is a
recurrent theme. Degas's paintings of ballet dancers in the late nineteenth century are followed by an early twentieth-century obsession
with dance which is less concerned with documentation and ostensible
subject matter and more with dance as a metaphor for some aspect
of the modern world.[20] For Futurism, with its passion for the ma-
chine and the dynamism of the modern city, dance can stand for the
frantic mobility of the new century.[21] Gino Severini painted a series
of Dancers, intended to capture movement and light (plate 4).[22] The
Vorticist painter and writer Percy Wyndham Lewis, in the English
version of Futurism, also employed the image of the dancer in his

5   Percy Wyndham Lewis, *Kermesse*, 1912, bodycolour, pen and black
ink, watercolour with traces of graphite, 35 × 35.1 cms. Yale Center
for British Art, Museum Purchase (Paul Mellon Fund and Gift of
Neil F. and Ivan E. Phillips in memory of their mother,
Mrs Rosalie Phillips).

work (plate 5). For Henri Matisse, the dancer exemplifies both his
paramount stress on the human figure and his search for serenity
(plate 6).[23] In addition, the modernist construction of 'the primitive'
plays a part in this focus on the dance. In the case of Expressionism,
for example in the paintings of Emil Nolde and Ernst Ludwig Kirchner
(plate 7) and the expressionistic work of the Fauve artist, André
Derain, the dancer is a common figure, often invoked to represent
the image of authenticity and purity in the face of the supposed

6 Henri Matisse, *Dance (I)*, 1909, oil on canvas, 259.1 × 390.1 cms.
The Museum of Modern Art, New York. Gift of Nelson Rockefeller
in honour of Alfred H. Barr, Jnr. © Succession H. Matisse/DACS,
London, 1995; Artists Rights Society (ARS), New York
© 1992, The Museum of Modern Art.

materialism and alienation of the modern world.[24] In the abstract
and mechanical figures of dance produced by Mondrian and other
De Stijl artists, a notion of the primitive and the exotic was similarly
in play.[25] Rodin's interest in the dance (he spent time drawing in
Isadora Duncan's dance school in Paris in 1906 and made a series
of drawings and a sculpture of Nijinsky in 1912) included a particular attraction to Javanese dance; in 1908 he also made a number of
heads of the Japanese dancer Hanako.[26] Why the dancer figures so
importantly in the texts of modernism is a complicated question:
here I will only suggest that the timing had a good deal to do with
the culmination of a long period during which the body was culturally suppressed.[27] It is no coincidence that in a culture in which the
corporeal has been progressively repressed the metaphoric locus of
social revolt is the body. I also believe that, despite the cultural

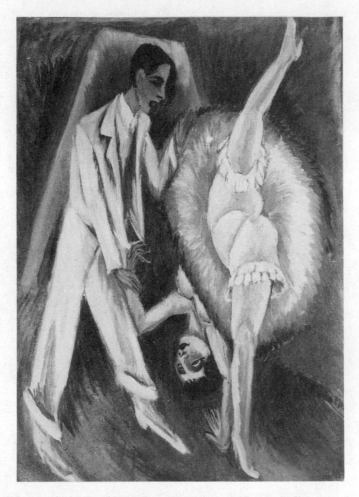

7   Ernst Ludwig Kirchner, *Dancer*, 1912. Museum Folkwang, Essen.

revolutions of the 1920s and the 1960s, we inherit this notion that the body is both the ground of cultural (and gender) oppression and the potential site of its overthrow. The current enthusiasm for the work of Bakhtin, and for the notions of the carnivalesque and the grotesque body, I think bear witness to this.

In the late twentieth century, then, we find many examples of the argument that dance is the real or metaphorical arena of liberation. Elizabeth Dempster writes that 'the body, dancing, can challenge and deconstruct cultural inscription . . . In moments of dancing the edges of things blur and terms such as mind/body, flesh/spirit, carnal/ divine, male/female become labile and unmoored, breaking loose from the fixing of their pairings.'[28] Judith Lynne Hanna quotes approvingly David Holmstrom's comment that 'if Richard Nixon had known how to dance . . . Watergate would not have happened',[29] making the more general claim that 'dance is a unique way to convey messages of identity: generational difference, gender, ethnicity, and social class. Messages in motion are also about desire and fantasy, defiance and anger'.[30] (She fails to explain how this Terpsichorean expression produces such responsible politics.) And Angela McRobbie has explored the role of dance (classical and modern, performance and social) in the fantasy lives of girls and women, suggesting that 'dance has always offered a channel, albeit a limited one, for bodily self-expression and control; it has also been a source of pleasure and sensuality'.[31] Young girls identify with the fictional careers of ballerinas and other dancers (including those in film narratives like *Flashdance* and *Fame*) or participate in the autonomy and self-absorption of social dance. In considering particularly the freedoms dance offers to girls, McRobbie is also well aware of the limits of these freedoms and of the less progressive aspects of these phenomena: the woman dancer as object of the voyeuristic gaze, the real constraints on the lives of working-class teenage girls, from which the dance hall provides only a temporary release. But here, as in the other texts, the possibility of transgression is seen to reside in the dancing body.

It is on the basis of this assumption that dance has operated as a metaphor in cultural criticism, to signify other kinds of freedoms and transgressions – textual, linguistic and social. When we look more closely, it turns out that the *way* in which dance functions is rather unstable. Criticism that is like dance may be so for a number of reasons: because it is joyful or playful; because it is grounded in the body; because it is thought to circumvent language; because the critic believes identities are mobile rather than fixed. Sometimes more than one notion is in play in the same metaphor. But these analogies are rarely thought out. In none of these senses, I believe, does the trope of theory-as-dance achieve the desired end of identifying either a better critical practice or a useful cultural politics. To show this, I want to look more closely at some examples of this 'dance criticism', to discover the basis on which they propose this metaphor of mobility.

Annette Kolodny's 1980 essay, 'Dancing through the minefield', was an important and much anthologized contribution to feminist literary criticism; it introduced the metaphor of dance to express a hope that feminist critics may proceed to work together amicably and productively, despite theoretical and other differences.[32] Confronted with the growing diversity of approach and focus (rediscovery of women's writing, critique of men's writing, analysis of literature as institution and so on), Kolodny recommends a 'playful pluralism' by feminists, dedicated to examine the constitution of our own aesthetics and reading practices by the eclectic use of multiple critical approaches. The minefield of conflict or of lack of coherence can be avoided by such a pluralism. The idea of dance appears only in the very last sentence: ('. . . so that others, after us, may literally dance through the minefield'[33]), but it is, of course, picked up and given prominence in the essay's title, which promotes dancing as the way forward for feminist critics. The essay was quickly subjected to some severe criticism – for its minimizing of important differences within feminism, its failure to recognize the total incompatibility of certain approaches and, most importantly, its exclusion of issues of sexual orientation and ethnicity.[34] In addition, the elegance of dance has seemed to some to be too feminine and delicate a mode of operating; as Marcus put it, 'It is far too early to tear down the barricades. Dancing shoes will not do. We still need our heavy boots and mine detectors.'[35] But the idea that feminist criticism is something like dancing has remained attractive and has been taken up by other writers – most recently by Nancy Miller, who again foregrounds it in the title of her essay 'Dreaming, dancing, and the changing locations of feminist criticism',[36] in order to consider the issues involved in the employment of this metaphor by Kolodny and other feminists. Miller also discusses another important source of the metaphor in feminist and cultural criticism, namely the 1981 interview with Derrida published in *Diacritics* the following year',[37] and I want to turn to this now.

While Kolodny's notion of theory-as-dance simply registers a commitment to liberal pluralism, its meaning for Derrida and those who have taken up his concept of 'incalculable choreographies' seems to inhere in the very mobility of the dance. In response to a question about the nature and possibilities of sexual difference, Derrida's reply is to suggest that we can go beyond binary divisions, 'beyond the opposition feminine/masculine, beyond bisexuality as well, beyond

homosexuality and heterosexuality which come to the same thing'.[38]
The view that sexuality and gender are not fixed in a binary divide
has been important in recent work by Judith Butler, Biddy Martin,
Marjorie Garber and others working in gay and lesbian studies.[39]
Derrida's 'dream of the innumerable' similarly suggests the arbitrari-
ness of the social and psychic 'fixing' of gender identities. Susan
Suleiman takes this up, with Derrida's notion of 'incalculable choreographies', not from the point of view of gay studies but as a
feminist project of writing 'beyond the number two'.[40] She discusses
Angela Carter's novel *The Passion of the New Eve* as an example
of a text that engages, like Virginia Woolf's *Orlando*, in a narrative
of sexual indeterminacy, sex-changes and fluctuating gender identity. Miller is less enthusiastic about such a dismantling of binaries.
She puts it like this:

> To be sure, for a feminism focused on the question of sexual differ-
> ence and difference in language, the dream of the innumerable figures
> a dance of playful possibility. And why shouldn't feminists have fun?
> But at the same time, it is, I think, the exclusive emphasis in decon-
> structive and feminist rhetorics on a radically decontextualized sexual
> difference that has papered over – with extremely serious consequences
> – both the institutional and political differences between men and
> women and the equally powerful social and cultural differences between
> women.[41]

This is both an analytic and a political critique of 'choreography'
as a model for theory, which insists at the same time on the persistent structural divisions in society and on the strategic necessity to
mobilize on the basis of these. But I am interested in asking a different question. Why is it that the concepts of 'dance' (which recurs
throughout the interview with Derrida) and 'choreographies' are
employed to do the work of radical destabilization? It is not enough
to observe that dance is movement and is therefore on the side of the
critique of stasis: walking, marching and swimming are also forms
of movement, though they do not seem to offer themselves as metaphors in the same way. Two specific assumptions about dance, both
of them questionable, explain its attraction as a trope in critical
theory: first, that dance, being non-verbal or pre-verbal, bypasses
language in its signifying practice – it thus subverts (phal)logocentrism;
second, that dance, being grounded in the body, provides access to
what is repressed in culture. Because, unlike walking and swimming,

dance is perceived as creative, it is seen to articulate the authentic expressions of the body. From these assumptions the conclusions are drawn that dance is or may be liberating and, *a fortiori*, that metaphors of dance operate automatically as critical theory.

Sandra Kemp has recently argued that dance criticism operates with 'too simple a binary opposition between the intellect and the senses'.[42] She insists on the complex 'intersections of speech, writing, text and body (the reflexive relations of dance and language)',[43] and suggests that in *all* dance 'the intellect' and language are already implicated and inscribed. It may be the case that dance cannot easily be translated into words, but, as she says, this does not mean that dance is somehow 'outside' language.[44] These facts are obvious: that dance is taught at least partly 'in words'; that many forms of performance dance, especially in the classical and modern repertoires, tell stories which are based on verbal or written narratives, including those written in the programme notes; that it is quite common in post-modern dance for words to play a part in the performance. But it is finally also the case that the dancing body is that of the human, social and hence language-using person. The experience of dance, by its performers or by its audiences, can never be an experience outside language.

It is interesting, in fact, that the notion of dance as liberating or deconstructive has also been used metaphorically in relation to language. Elsewhere Derrida quotes Nietzsche's proposal that the writer should learn 'to dance with the *pen*'.[45] Here, rather than the suggestion that to dance is to escape the constraints of linguistic rationality, we find the idea that language itself can be rendered innovative and critical by learning to write, think and speak in the mode of the dance.[46] Françoise Meltzer sees Salome's dance, in its various textual appearances, as 'a metaphor for writing in the logocentric perspective', in which the blind spot of writing to its own repression is confronted.[47] Although this is, of course, a literal reference to a dance, to Salome's dance, her argument is actually about a 'dancing' language and writing. The 'dance of the pen' (Nietzsche's phrase, which she also cites) has to do with *any* unspecified writing strategies that destabilize meaning.

The idea of dance as unmediated bodily expression is as suspect as the idea of extra-linguistic experience. This notion has had some currency in recent years, and not just in dance criticism. It can be traced to certain essays of Barthes, particularly 'The grain of the voice', in which he contrasts the 'pheno-song' (expressive, proficient, dramatic, but lacking in 'grain', in the materiality of the body) with the 'geno-song' ('the body in the voice as it sings', bringing *jouissance*).[48] This concept of a direct engagement with the corporeal has been taken up with enthusiasm in some areas of cultural studies. In feminist criticism, Hélène Cixous's work has also been influential in the development of a politics of the body, including some versions of the concept of an *écriture féminine*. In the now famous phrases of her exhortation to women writers, Cixous says, 'by writing her self, women will return to the body which has been more than confiscated from her. . . . Censor the body and you censor breath and speech at the same time . . . Write your self. Your body must be heard'.[49] A feminism which emphasizes the primacy of the body in writing is bound to identify the potential of the dancing body.[50] On this question, I endorse Georgina Born's dismissal of what she calls 'a particularly barren, banal and overworked aspect of post-structuralist theory: the concept of jouissance, and the tired insistence on the body'.[51] As she shows, these 'ineffable' areas of liberation do not stand up at all to analysis, but operate vaguely, unhistorically and, in the end, uselessly.

Just as there can be no pre-linguistic experience, so there is no pre-social experience of the body. Nor does it follow from the fact that the body is the site of repression that using the body in certain ways thereby overthrows the structures of that repression. In any case, a knowledge of how dance works makes it clear that there is nothing unmediated going on here. A good deal of dance, especially performance (as opposed to social) dance, is thoroughly mediated by cultural languages and practices: it is often notated and recorded; it is usually choreographed; it can be highly formalized. Susan Leigh Foster's detailed account of the technical skills and training involved in various forms of dance puts paid to any idea that there is something natural or intuitive about it.[52] She undertakes this demonstration of how dancing bodies are *created* as a counter to recent critical writings. 'These writings seldom address the body I know; instead, they move quickly past arms, legs, torso and head on their way to a theoretical agenda that requires something unknowable or unknown as an initial premise. The body remains mysterious and ephemeral, a convenient receptacle for their new theoretical positions.'[53] There *is* no immediate body. Indeed, Foster shows that the bodies produced by different dance techniques – ballet, Duncan,

Graham, Cunningham and contact improvisation – are specific to those techniques. So there is no generic 'dancing body' either. And although, in the case of social dance or untrained performance dance, the body is not 'produced' in the same way, it is important to insist that even here the movement is socially learned. That is, even where there is no sustained or professional training in dance technique, dancing is still coded, stylized and appropriated in social and cultural contexts.

In a way, the metaphor of dance as a kind of cultural criticism is appealing, inasmuch as it signifies an elegant, creative non-linear movement of thought. I have been arguing against the assumption that this movement is uncontrolled, natural, pre-cultural and/or intrinsically subversive or progressive. At the very least, I have tried to show that this is the assumption that lies behind the somewhat promiscuous use of dance metaphors in feminist and other cultural criticism. There is clearly something very persuasive about the idea of the free and dancing body. I conclude with a different visual image, the work of the dance photographer Lois Greenfield[54] (plate 8). It seems, as well as any images I know, to capture the spontaneity and freedom of dance; yet it does not in fact record a moment in dance. Every shot she takes is constructed in the photographer's studio. As she explains, she prefers to work on her own terms, with dancers who are prepared to leap and pose in this way. It has nothing to do with choreography, and little to do with dance, except inasmuch as these are the bodies of trained dancers. To me, her 'dance' photographs illustrate very well the case I have been trying to make – that we understand very little about dance when we make the too easy assumption that to dance is to be free, and that this freedom is immediately visible. What is made clear here is the way we tend to carry around our cultural prejudices about the meaning of dance. Once we realize that this is not an image of dance, we are also forced to reconsider our notion that we perceive dance in a particular way. For although inappropriate dancing (by Nora or the Mundy sisters for example) can be a rebellious act, dance in itself is no different from other kinds of social practice.

For this reason, I have been delighted to see that the work of critical theory, feminism and cultural studies is at last being taken up by dance scholars.[55] Dance, like music, has remained resistant to social-historical critique, and it seems likely that the demystifying project of critical dance studies will help to demolish the kinds of

8   Lois Greenfield, *Bill T. Jones/Arnie Zane & Company*, 1983,
Breaking Bounds, plate no. 69. From William A. Ewing, *Breaking
Bounds: The Dance Photographs of Lois Greenfield*, Thames &
Hudson Ltd., London and Chronicle Books, San Francisco,
1992. © Lois Greenfield, 1983.

myths about dance which I have considered here. Maybe the metaphor
of choreography works better than that of dance, as it too registers
the possibility of a different, non-linear movement, but does not pretend to endorse a claim of ungrounded, unconstrained mobility. In
any case, it is time to stop allowing a romantic, pre-critical conception
of dance to act as an illegitimate short cut to cultural analysis.

NOTES

1   Interview with Donal Donnelly, who played Father Jack in both the
Dublin and the New York productions, Playbill vol. 92, no. 1, Plymouth Theatre (January 1992), p. 10.

2　*Dancing at Lughnasa* (Faber and Faber, 1990), p. 1.

3　Ibid., p. 22.

4　Ibid., p. 71.

5　The play had transferred, with most of its original cast, from the Abbey Theatre, Dublin, where it premièred on 24 April 1990.

6　I am struck by the number of books by women authors, fiction and non-fiction, feminist and non-feminist, with 'dance' in their titles: Margaret Atwood's *Dancing Girls*, Joan Barfoot's *Dancing in the Dark*, Janet Hobhouse's *Dancing in the Dark*, Ursula LeGuin's *Dancing at the Edge of the World*, for example. Andrew Holleran's *Dancer from the Dancer* is a different but related case, in which dance and the metaphor of dance figure importantly in the portrayal of male gay life in New York in the 1970s.

7　Sandra Kemp has also recently noted this use of the dance metaphor in literary theory: 'Conflicting choreographies: Derrida and dance', *New Formations*, no. 16, Spring 1992.

8　For example, Jane Desmond, 'Dancing out the difference: cultural imperialism and Ruth St Denis's "Radha" ', *Signs*, vol. 17, no. 1 (Autumn 1991); Angela McRobbie, 'Dance and social fantasy', in Angela McRobbie and Mica Nava (eds), *Gender and Generation* (Macmillan, 1984); Judith Lynne Hanna: 'Moving messages: identity and desire in popular music and social dance', in James Lull (ed.), *Popular Music and Communication*, 2nd edn (Sage, 1992). See also Helen Thomas (ed.), *Dance, Gender and Culture* (Macmillan, 1993).

9　*A Doll's House* was written in 1879.

10　Henrik Ibsen, *A Doll's House* (Eyre Methuen, 1980), p. 77.

11　Jane Marcus, 'Salomé: the Jewish princess was a new woman', in *Art and Anger. Reading like a Woman* (Ohio State University Press, 1988), p. 12.

12　Ibid., p. 8. Richard Ellmann reads Wilde's counterposition of the pure and puritanical Iokanaan (John the Baptist) with the sensual Salome as a literary translation of that between John Ruskin and Walter Pater, both of whom he admired: 'Overtures to "Salome"', in *Golden Codgers: Biographical Speculations*, Oxford University Press, 1973.

13　Françoise Meltzer, *Salome and the Dance of Writing* (University of Chicago Press, 1987), p. 33. See also Linda Seidel, 'Salome and the canons', *Women's Studies*, vol. 11 (1984).

14　Written in 1891.

15　Oscar Wilde, *Salome* (Faber and Faber, 1989), p. 54.

16　The music for the dance was composed in 1905, a couple of months after the rest of the opera. The longer scenario for the Dance dates from the 1920s. See Derrick Puffett, *Richard Strauss: Salome* (Cambridge University Press, 1989), p. 165.

17   J.-K. Huysmans, *Against Nature* (Penguin, 1959 [1884]), p. 64.

18   Ibid., p. 66.

19   This is not necessarily the case for all contemporary visual images of Salome: for example, Klimt's *Judith II: Salome* (1909) and Munch's *Salome* (1894–8) both portray the woman (as destroyer) but not the dance.

20   I am taking Degas's images as simply showing a straightforward interest in dance and dancers (as opposed to symbols of something other than dance) and hence as a kind of documentation. However, Richard Kendall has recently shown that although Degas's images of dancers from the 1870s are realistic in their attention to detail, those from the 1890s are much less detailed and informative: 'Signs and non-signs: Degas' changing strategies of representation', in Richard Kendall and Griselda Pollock (eds), *Dealing with Degas: Representations of Women and the Politics of Vision* (Universe, 1992).

21   As one Futurist manifesto put it, 'Universal dynamism must be rendered in painting as a dynamic sensation': *Futurist Painting: Technical Manifesto*, 11 April 1910, reproduced in Herschel B. Chipp, *Theories of Modern Art* (University of California Press, 1968), p. 289.

22   Caroline Tisdall, *Futurism* (Thames and Hudson, 1977), p. 53.

23   Chipp, *Theories of Modern Art*, p. 125.

24   On Nolde's relationship to primitivism, see Jill Lloyd, 'Emil Nolde's "ethnographic" still lifes: primitivism, tradition, and modernity', in Susan Hiller (ed.), *The Myth of Primitivism: Perspectives on Art* (Routledge, 1991). On modernism and primitivism more generally, see also Marianna Torgovnick, *Gone Primitive: Savage Intellects, Modern Lives* (University of Chicago Press, 1990); Hal Foster: 'The "primitive" unconscious of modern art, or white skin black masks', in his *Recodings* (Bay Press, 1985).

25   Nancy J. Troy, 'Figures of the dance in De Stijl', *The Art Bulletin*, vol. LXVI, no. 4 (December 1984). Thanks to Mark Cheetham for this reference.

26   John L. Tancock, *The Sculpture of Auguste Rodin* (David R. Godine/ Philadelphia Museum of Art, 1976), pp. 82, 83, 85. It is not clear why he only modelled Hanako's head, since Tancock quotes him as particularly taken with her dancing body: 'Her muscles are clean-cut and prominent like those of a fox-terrier . . . Her anatomy is quite different from that of Europeans, but is very beautiful, and has extraordinary power' (p. 546). See also Joy Newton: 'Rodin and Nijinsky', *Gazette des Beaux-Arts*, vol. 114 (September 1989).

27   See, for example, Francis Barker, *The Tremulous Private Body: Essays on Subjection* (Methuen, 1984); Peter Stallybrass and Allon White, *The Politics and Poetics of Transgression* (Methuen, 1986).

28   Elizabeth Dempster, 'Women writing the body: let's watch a little how she dances', in Susan Sheridan (ed.), *Grafts. Feminist Cultural Criticism* (Verso, 1988), pp. 50, 52.
29   Hanna, 'Moving messages', p. 191, quoting David Holmstrom, 'Dancing at the White House', *Christian Science Monitor*, 1988 April 22, p. 14.
30   Hanna, 'Moving messages', p. 176.
31   McRobbie, 'Dance and social fantasy', pp. 132–3.
32   Annette Kolodny, 'Dancing through the minefield: some observations on the theory, practice and politics of a feminist literary criticism', *Feminist Studies*, vol. 6, no. 1 (Spring 1980), reprinted in Mary Eagleton (ed.), *Feminist Literary Theory: A Reader* (Basil Blackwell, 1986) and in Elaine Showalter (ed.), *The New Feminist Criticism: Essays on Women, Literature and Theory* (Virago Press, 1986).
33   Kolodny, 'Dancing through the minefield', p. 22.
34   See responses in *Feminist Studies*, vol. 8, no. 3 (Fall 1982), by Judith Kegan Gardiner, Elly Bulkin and Rena Grasso Patterson.
35   Jane Marcus, 'Storming the toolshed', in Nannerl O. Keohane, Michelle Z. Rosaldo, and Barbara C. Gelpi (eds), *Feminist Theory: A Critique of Ideology* (Harvester Press, 1982).
36   Nancy Miller, 'Dreaming, dancing, and the changing locations of feminist criticism, 1988', in *Getting Personal* (Routledge, 1991).
37   Jacques Derrida and Christie V. McDonald, 'Choreographies', *Diacritics*, vol. 12 (1982).
38   Ibid., p. 76.
39   Judith Butler, *Gender Trouble: Feminism and the Subversion of Identity* (Routledge, 1990) and 'Imitation and gender insubordination', in Diana Fuss (ed.), *Inside/Out: Lesbian Theories, Gay Theories* (Routledge, 1991); Biddy Martin: 'Sexual practice and changing lesbian identities', in Michèle Barrett and Anne Phillips (eds), *Destabilizing Theory: Contemporary Feminist Debates* (Polity Press, 1992); Marjorie Garber, *Vested Interests: Cross-Dressing and Cultural Anxiety* (Routledge, Chapman and Hall, 1992).
40   Susan Rubin Suleiman, '(Re)writing the body: the politics and poetics of female eroticism', in Susan Rubin Suleiman (ed.), *The Female Body in Western Culture* (Harvard University Press, 1986), p. 24.
41   Miller, 'Dreaming, dancing', p. 80.
42   Kemp, 'Conflicting choreographies', p. 95. See also her articles, '"Let's watch a little how he dances" – performing cultural studies', *Critical Quarterly*, vol. 34, no. 1 (Spring 1992), and 'But what if the object began to speak? The aesthetics of dance', in Andrew Benjamin and Peter Osborne (eds), *Thinking Art: Beyond Traditional Aesthetics* (Institute of Contemporary Arts, London, 1991). Some of the same material is covered in these three articles.

43 Kemp, 'Conflicting choreographies', p. 94.
44 Simon Frith makes a similar argument about music, 'Adam Smith and Music', *New Formations*, no. 18 (Winter 1992). Frith considers an analysis of the experience of music as a combination of the intellectual and the sensual: 'listening means grasping a piece intellectually and then taking sensual pleasure in the "movement" of the mind' (p. 80).
45 Jacques Derrida, 'Force and signification', in *Writing and Difference* (Routledge & Kegan Paul, 1978), p. 29; Friedrich Nietzsche, *Twilight of the Idols* (Penguin, 1968), p. 66.
46 Vincent Leitch explores this issue in the work of J. Hillis Miller, 'The lateral dance: the deconstructive criticism of J. Hillis Miller', *Critical Inquiry*, vol. 6, no. 4 (Summer 1980).
47 Meltzer, *Salome and the Dance of Writing*, pp. 45–6.
48 Roland Barthes, 'The grain of the voice', in *Image-Music-Text* (Fontana, 1977).
49 Hélène Cixous, 'The laugh of the Medusa', reprinted in Elaine Marks and Isabelle de Courtivron (eds), *New French Feminisms* (Schocken Books, 1981), p. 250.
50 Luce Irigaray, another 'French feminist', has suggested a crucial link between femininity and dance. In relation to Freud's discussion of the *fort-da* game, she points out that the girl does not play the same game in relation to the mother's absence. Instead, she refuses to speak and eat; she plays with a doll; and 'she dances, thereby constructing for herself a vital subjective space. . . . This dance is also a way of creating for herself her own territory in relation to the mother.' ('The gesture in psychoanalysis', in Teresa Brennan (ed.), *Between Feminism and Psychoanalysis* (Routledge, 1989), p. 132.) I suppose this is the kind of statement that gets taken up in relation to a politics of the body; but it is not one I find very convincing.
51 Georgina Born, 'Women, music, politics, difference: Susan McClary's *Feminine Endings: Music, Gender and Sexuality*', *Women: a Cultural Review*, vol. 3, no. 1 (1992), pp. 83–4. Her specific criticism is of McClary's approval of Madonna and the *jouissance* of her music.
52 Susan Leigh Foster, 'Dancing bodies', in Jonathan Crary and Sanford Kwinter (eds), *Incorporations* (Urzone, 1992).
53 Ibid., p. 480.
54 Lois Greenfield, *Breaking Bounds* (Thames and Hudson, 1992).
55 See note 8.

6

The Artist and the Flâneur: *Rodin, Rilke and Gwen John in Paris*

Rodin's Muse

Room 14 in the Rodin Museum in Paris is devoted to sculptures designed for various public monuments. Behind a large study for a monument of Balzac are two small pieces, both identified as studies for a statue planned for London in honour of the artist Whistler: a marble head of 1905, and a small bronze figure on a pedestal, *La Muse* of 1904–5[1] (plate 9). This commission was never completed, though there are numerous sketches and plaster and bronze studies which relate to the project. The model for the figure was the Welsh artist Gwen John, who had come to Paris in 1904 and met Rodin soon after her arrival.

I have been interested in the relative invisibility of Gwen John in accounts of the lives of certain famous men. She puts in a marginal appearance in relation, particularly, to four people: her brother, the artist Augustus John; her employer, friend and lover Rodin; the poet Rainer Maria Rilke, who was also working for Rodin in the 1900s; and the New York collector John Quinn, who was her sole and reliable patron from 1910 until his death in 1924.[2] Three of them thought highly of her work, John Quinn and her brother working actively to promote it and to encourage her. Augustus John, far better known and more successful than his sister in their lifetime, predicted that 'fifty years after my death I shall be remembered as

9 Auguste Rodin, *Muse for the Monument to Whistler*, 1904–5,
bronze, 65.5 × 33 × 34 cms. Photograph Bruno Jarret/ADAGP
and copyright Musée Rodin, Paris. © ADAGP, Paris and
DACS, London, 1994.

Gwen John's brother'.[3] Rodin admired her work: she told her brother
that he had said 'vous êtes belle artiste'.[4] (Rodin was generous in his
support of younger women artists. Camille Claudel, his great passion in the 1880s, was a talented sculptor, whose work he promoted
energetically. According to Rodin's express wish in 1917, a room at
the Rodin Museum in Paris is devoted to her work and to work of
Rodin's inspired by her.[5]) Despite Gwen John's own diffidence, re-
luctance to exhibit and chronic unreliability in fulfilling commissions
from Quinn, she is now recognized as a major artist, probably both

as a by-product of twenty years of feminist revisionism and as a result of the ever growing demands of the art market.[6]

Her marginality to the stories of Rodin and Rilke is not particularly surprising given her notorious reclusiveness and her virtual invisibility as an artist in the 1900s. In Donald Prater's biography of Rilke, for example, she is mentioned only once, as one of the younger artists Rilke met during his years with Rodin.[7] And because, as far as we know, she was the model for only one of Rodin's sculptures, she rates only a passing mention in Albert Elsen's study of Rodin's work.[8] She lived a very solitary existence, with few friends and confidantes.[9] She kept her distance from group avant-garde life in Paris,[10] though a work of hers, owned by John Quinn, was included in the 1913 Armory Show (plate 10), and she attended a dinner given by Quinn in Paris in 1923 in the company of Brancusi and other modern artists whom Quinn patronized.[11] In addition, it is clear that she was far less important to Rodin than he was to her. For over ten years, from 1904, the year she moved to Paris and became involved with him, until his death in 1917, he was her obsession. She wrote him about two thousand letters (now collected in the Rodin Museum in Paris), and organized her day around his visits, cancelling sittings by her own models if necessary.[12] On his side, she soon became his *cinq-à-sept*, and although he continued to visit her and to show concern for her health and welfare, she was displaced in his affections by the Duchesse de Choiseul. Towards the end of his life, she was refused entry to his home.[13] So although the discovery and reassessment of her work is bound to produce new narratives about her contemporaries in which she plays more than a minor role, it is not simply a matter of citing gender prejudice either on the part of those contemporaries, because they had none, or on the part of biographers and historians, who have merely recorded Gwen John's actual significance in their subjects' lives.

I am interested in exploring here, therefore, the structures of exclusion that did operate to marginalize Gwen John in the artistic life of Paris in the 1900s. I shall discuss her in relation to her contemporary and friend Rainer Maria Rilke, both in terms of their different access to Rodin and to public life, and in terms of their respective work, which appears, at least on the surface, to register this difference. It is always risky to take individual figures as typical of a wider social group, and, given the eccentric characters and life-styles of both Rilke and John, I do not wish to make such claims here. In

10   Gwen John, *Girl Reading at a Window*, 1911, oil on canvas,
40.9 × 25.3 cms. The Museum of Modern Art, New York. Mary
Anderson Conroy Bequest in memory of her mother,
Julia Quinn Anderson.

addition, despite their similar situations in Paris (as artists, foreigners, employees of Rodin, amongst other things), there were important disparities of class and wealth which differentiated them.

However, I shall begin by discussing the way in which gender difference seems to parallel a public/private divide, which had to do not only with access to Rodin's studio, but also with access to the street. The case of Rilke and John supports the argument that *flânerie* is gendered.[14] I shall then consider potential challenges to this argument. The first is the empirical question: *were* women in fact seriously restricted in the public sphere? In particular, did Rilke and John pursue, respectively, such 'public' and 'private' lives? Secondly, I will look at recent work on gender (and sexual) identity, which has encouraged us to see such identity as more fluid and ambiguous, and then relate this to the specific gender identities of Rilke and John.

Lastly, I turn to the literature on social space (Lefebvre, de Certeau, urban geography), which has operated to destabilize the notion of fixed geographical and physical structures, emphasizing instead the social *meanings* of space and substituting a hermeneutics or phenomenology of space for a structural account. The question raised here is whether it then makes more sense to see John and Rilke negotiating public and private space in ways which may have been less rigid than the social history of 'separate spheres' suggests. Understanding the subtleties of gender and space ambiguity proves important in this case; but I intend to stress the limits of ambiguity, and the persistence and effectiveness of social categories and social/physical constraints, which did, in fact, structure the possibilities of Gwen John's life.

An interior life

As a reviewer of the 1985 Barbican exhibition of Gwen John's work points out, 'few foreign artists choosing to work in Paris so resolutely turned their backs on the city itself'.[15] Until she moved from Paris in 1911, to the suburbs at Meudon (near Rodin's own home), John never painted outdoor scenes. Her subjects are invariably self-portraits and portraits of women sitters in her own room in Paris (plate 11), or even simply the room itself (plate 12). The Barbican exhibition and the book published to accompany it, were entitled *Gwen John: An Interior Life*.[16] The phrase comes from a letter John

11 Gwen John, *La Chambre sur la Cour*, 1907–8, oil on canvas,
31 × 21.5 cms. Collection of Mr and Mrs Paul Mellon,
Upperville, Virginia.

12   Gwen John, *Interior*, 1915–16, oil on canvas, 33 × 24.2 cms.
© The Cleveland Museum of Art, Mr and Mrs William
H. Marlatt Fund, 82.6.

wrote in 1912 to her friend, Ursula Tyrwhitt, whom she had met at
the Slade School of Fine Art in the 1890s, and who remained her
closest confidante: 'As to whether I have anything worth expressing
that is apart from the question. I may never have anything to express, except this desire for a more interior life.'[17] To Rodin she
wrote, 'My room is so delicious after a whole day outside, it seems
to me that I am not myself except in my room'.[18] (Since she moved

several times, 'my room' is in fact a number of addresses in Montparnasse.[19]) *Girl Reading at a Window* of 1911 (plate 10) and *La Chambre sur la Cour* of 1907–8 (plate 11) are both self-portraits. In a letter to Rodin, John compares these works to Dutch seventeenth-century interiors.[20] They are small in scale (16 by 10 inches and $12\frac{1}{2}$ by $8\frac{1}{2}$ inches respectively), delicate in palette and intimate in mood. The ambiguity in John's statement of her desire for an 'interior life' (she was also attracted to the spiritual life, and converted to Roman Catholicism in 1913) only confirms her preference for the solitary and the private, in evidence in these two images of women alone and self-contained in their pursuit – reading and sewing. In addition, John actively hated being out on the streets of Paris. Susan Chitty records several occasions on which John had to retreat to her room, feeling herself harassed by *rôdeurs* or simply feeling too self-conscious.

> As the weather improved she sketched out of doors, for she had never lost her childhood habit of carrying a sketch-book. She drew classical statues in the Luxembourg gardens and Rodin's statues in the Luxembourg museum. . . . She became so embarrassed when sketching one morning on the boat to St Cloud that she decided to try and memorise the faces of the people she saw and draw them afterwards. The experiment was not a success and from this period there exist few drawings of strangers.[21]

Gwen John's singular focus on women and domestic interiors and her own statements about her more natural habitat accord well with a feminist history of separate spheres, which has explored the ways in which during the nineteenth century the bourgeois woman was increasingly limited in the social arena. The simple equation of men-public and women-private is, of course, quite wrong, for many reasons. Men also inhabited the private realm of the home. Working-class women always, and necessarily, traversed the public sphere of work and the street. The rise of the department store in the latter part of the nineteenth century provided a new and quite respectable semi-public arena for middle-class women, as did the park, the theatre and various other non-domestic spaces. Indeed, it is more the case that the *ideology* of separate spheres and of women's proper place was dominant, operating to render invisible (or unrespectable) women who were in the street. Nevertheless, there is no doubt that the lives of middle-class women were fairly circumscribed, both in terms of opportunities in the public sphere and by virtue of such social values. The equation of femininity with the domestic, though a distortion or at least an oversimplification of women's actual lives, has an important basis in the reality of their experience. Feminist art historians have therefore been right to read the work of women artists through this structuring of social space.[22]

Like the work of Mary Cassatt and Berthe Morisot, Gwen John's paintings represent the 'feminine' space of the home. Unlike that work, however, her images are never of groups of women, or of women and children.[23] Over and over again, she painted single women, single in both senses. The intimacy of an encounter, as in a Cassatt painting of women together or of a mother and child, is strongly present in John's work too. But there is a strange dislocation of the meaning of woman/feminine/domestic in the case of these lone figures who so clearly *refuse* women's mission – the roles of wife and mother. Exclusion from the public space is not compensated for in the inhabiting of the appropriate private space. In other words, it is difficult to read Gwen John's images in any straightforward way as participating in the representation and re-production of ideologies of gendered space.

There are other reasons to resist such a reading. Born and educated in Britain in the late Victorian period, John was of course a product of that age. But as an art student, a member of somewhat Bohemian circles in London and, later, an expatriate and an artist, John was clearly liberated from the values and demands of bourgeois life. In addition, her years in London and Paris coincided with the rise of the 'new woman' and of the women's suffrage movement, which created new possibilities for young women, especially those in the more avant-garde circles. In many ways, Gwen John's life was radically unfeminine with regard to her sexual relationships and lifestyle.[24] Moreover, the depiction of the domestic interior was not restricted to women. A number of writers have commented on the similarities between John's work and the 'intimist' paintings of Vuillard and Gilman, and the 'feminine' delicacy of colouring of Seurat.[25] Male artists, too, have worked in their rooms, even when the city itself has been their subject matter; Matisse and Chagall, for example, show Paris through the window rather than from within the street (plates 13 and 14). In other words, we cannot simply take Gwen John's work, in connection with a few of her quoted comments, as the unproblematic product of the disbarred *flâneuse*.

13   Henri Matisse, *A Glimpse of Notre Dame in the Late Afternoon*,
1902, oil on paper mounted on canvas, 71 × 54 cms. Albright-Knox
Art Gallery, Buffalo, New York. Gift of Seymour H. Knox, 1927.
© Succession H. Matisse/DACS, London, 1995.

14   Marc Chagall, *Paris Through the Window (Paris par la fenêtre)*,
1913, 135.8 × 141.4 cms. Solomon R. Guggenheim Museum, New
York. Gift, Solomon R. Guggenheim, 1937. Photo: Robert E. Mates.
© The Solomon R. Guggenheim Foundation, New York FN 37.438.
© ADAGP, Paris and DACS, London, 1995.

A city to die in

Gwen John first met Rilke at Rodin's studio in 1906. In 1908, they
met again, and became friends.[26] Augustus John describes this friendship as 'warm and close', noting that Rilke 'used to lend her books
and help her with his sympathy and understanding'.[27] Four of Rilke's
letters to her survive, written between 1908 and 1914 and 'intimate

in tone'.[28] Although after that they did not keep in close touch, she was greatly upset by his death in 1926; and on her own death a note addressed to him was found in her room, asking him to 'hold her hand and guide her when her brain slept'.[29] As with Rodin, however, her absence from biographies of Rilke seems to have been more a product of her relative unimportance to him than the result of selective narrative.

Rilke had originally come to Paris in 1902, to meet Rodin and to complete work on a monograph he was writing on the Master.[30] He left Paris early in 1903, travelling to Italy and back to Worpswede in Germany, where his wife, the sculptor Clara Westhoff, lived. After more travels in Italy and Sweden, he returned to Paris on 12 September 1905, to work as Rodin's secretary.[31] Although Rodin rather abruptly terminated his employment in May of the following year,[32] Rilke remained in Paris on and off, with many travels abroad, until 1911. Unlike Gwen John, he had free access to Rodin's studio and his home, meeting 'Mme. Rodin',[33] and eating meals with Rodin. While working as Rodin's secretary, he lived with him at the house in Meudon. Later, they both occupied rooms at the Hôtel Biron, at 77 rue de Varenne (now the Rodin Museum in Paris), which Rilke had discovered in 1908 and Rodin had first seen on visiting him there.

The street, as well as the studio, was available to Rilke in his discovery of Paris. His experience of public life, while not threatening in the way it was for Gwen John, was certainly not a pleasant one. In a letter written to his old friend and ex-lover Lou Andreas-Salomé in July 1903, he recalls the terror and fear he felt in the streets of Paris the year before:

> In August of last year I arrived there. It was the time when the trees in the city are withered without autumn, when the burning streets, expanded by the heat, will not end and one goes through smells as through many sad rooms. . . . When I passed by the Hôtel Dieu for the first time, an open carriage was just driving in, in which a person hung, swaying with every movement, askew like a broken marionette, and with a bad sore on his long, gray, dangling neck. And what people I met after that, almost every day; fragments of caryatids on whom the whole pain still lay, the entire structure of a pain, under which they were living slow as tortoises. And they were passers-by among passers-by, left alone and undisturbed in their fate. . . . And they were wearing the comfortless, discolored mimicry of the too

great cities, and were holding out under the foot of each day that trod
on them, like tough beetles, were enduring as if they still had to wait
for something, twitching like bits of a big chopped-up fish that is
already rotting but still alive.[34]

To Otto Modersohn, he wrote:

> Stick to your own country! Paris . . . is a difficult, difficult, anxious city.
> And the beautiful things there are here do not quite compensate . . . for
> what one must suffer from the cruelty and confusion of the streets
> and the monstrosity of the gardens, people, and things.[35]

He describes visits to Notre Dame, to the Louvre, to art exhibitions,
yet still, in 1907, adds that 'the difficult, the anxious is somehow
still here too – . . . as always in Paris'.[36]

In his only novel, *The Notebooks of Malte Laurids Brigge*, generally agreed to be quite autobiographical,[37] Rilke recreates the Paris
of his first experience, quoting liberally from his own letter to Salomé.
The book begins: 'So this is where people come to live; I would have
thought it is a city to die in.'[38] He goes on to describe the horrors
of the street sights of poverty and sickness, raucous noises invading
his room, the dreadfulness of silence. (The book then reverts to a
memoir of Malte's childhood and youth in Denmark.)

Rilke's Paris, then, is the public city, split for him between, on the
one hand, the beauty of its monuments and the endless opportunities to visit galleries and see great works and, on the other hand, the
anxiety and fear produced by being in the street. Rilke is the compulsive but reluctant *flâneur*. His fictional expression of his *flânerie*
in the Malte *Notebooks* is the equivalent of Gwen John's images of
domestic space, which equally record her own compulsive habitat.
Yet one could say that Rilke's Paris is no more real than John's, that
he too turned his back on the city. For, as is very clear, his relationship with the city and the street was highly neurotic.[39] Naomi Segal
has suggested that Rilke's 'Paris' is nothing other than a projection
of his own childhood fears, and that his writings about the city, in
letters and poetry as well as in the Malte *Notebooks*, operated for
him as a kind of therapy, a 'writing cure'.[40] As she says, in Rilke's
work we see nothing of the political mood or modern appearance of
the city, but rather the unreal, Baudelairean fantasy which is the
work of a distorting imagination.

So gender difference is not so clear cut, since what we confront here is not the public life of Rilke in contrast to the interior life of Gwen John, but rather a different kind of interior life, exteriorized onto the streets of Paris. I shall discuss Rilke's feminine characteristics and Gwen John's masculine characteristics later, in relation to the issue of gender ambiguity. Here, we see that manifestations of the public and the private, in social experience and in representation, cannot simply be mapped onto gender difference.

Gender and flânerie

How far was it the case that the Paris of the 1900s impeded women as *flâneuses*? There is some evidence that by that period some of the constraints of earlier decades had been removed.[41] Anne Friedberg suggests that as the department store supplanted the arcade, 'space opened for a female *flâneur* – a *flâneuse*', since shopping provided the possibility for women to wander the city alone.[42] Christopher Prendergast also identifies window-shopping as *flânerie*.[43] Naomi Schor, in her study of postcard images of Paris in 1900, finds evidence of the breakdown of systems of gender segregation, for example the visibility of women coach drivers, symbolizing, as she puts it, 'a new age of female urban mobility'.[44] And Adrian Rifkin raises the possibility of a 'feminist *flâneur*', whose gaze falls on a pretty man in the street.[45] Particularly for women of the less conventional circles of the art world, it seems that walking in the streets of Paris was not the outrageous or dangerous activity that persistent bourgeois gender codes implied. Two decades earlier the young Russian artist Marie Bashkirtseff was already recording in her journal her excursions in the city:

Wednesday, December 30 [1879] . . . On leaving the studio to-day I went to the Magasin du Louvre. It would take a Zola to describe this excited, busy, disgusting crowd, running, pushing, with heads thrust forward and eager eyes. I felt ready to faint from heat and weakness.

Monday, July 21 [1884] I walked for more than four hours today in search of a background for my picture; it is to be a street, but I have not yet fixed on the particular spot.[46]

Indeed, in spite of her unpleasant experiences in the streets, Gwen John often had opportunities to explore the exterior life. In one letter to Rodin, she describes going into the streets of Paris, to the Gare Montparnasse and in and out of a number of churches, in search of subjects for drawings.[47] When her cat was lost, in the summer of 1906, she slept outdoors for over a week in the town of Saint-Cloud, on the outskirts of Paris, hoping to find her. On a number of occasions she waited near the station, to meet Rodin on his arrival in Paris from Meudon, or waited outside his studio in order to walk with him to the station. She also continued to do some occasional outdoor sketching, for example in the Gare Montparnasse.[48]

In the early twentieth century, however, *flânerie* was still very much a gendered activity. As Priscilla Ferguson points out, shopping and window-shopping do not constitute *flânerie*, because the desire for the object on display rules out the necessary distance which characterizes the *flâneur*'s relationship to the public sphere.[49] Also, the shopper is engaged in a kind of purposive mobility which has nothing to do with the detached and aimless strolling of the *flâneur*. Inasmuch as the shopper is a woman, any deviation from the evidence of such purpose immediately renders her suspect – a loiterer, an unrespectable woman. To say that women come to have acceptable reasons to be in the street is not to identify them as *flâneuses*. For, as Rifkin also points out, 'the glance on the city is structured through gender as well as by it',[50] a reality which is in no way negated by the woman's sight of a 'pretty man'. Schor, too, makes it clear that in the Paris of 1900, despite the novelty of women drivers, there was still no female equivalent of the *flâneur*. In that period there were no real physical changes in the organization of the city which might have facilitated new gender arrangements. After its moment of revolutionary transformation in the second half of the nineteenth century, there followed a period of relative stasis. Apart from the growth of suburbs and the expansion of systems of transportation in the city (trams, motorbuses and eventually the Metro being added to existing modes of transport like the horse-drawn omnibus and horse-drawn tram), there was little modernization in Paris in the period 1890–1940, and little in the way of major planning and physical restructuring.[51] If anything, the increase in suburbanization could be assumed to have compounded the 'separation of spheres' in middle-class lives, as it had done in an earlier period in England.[52] Certainly, there is no evidence that the pressure of gender ideology had abated. Even Marie Bashkirtseff's sketching expeditions in Paris seem to have been undertaken sometimes from within her carriage – where she was also harassed by people in the street and forced to return home. On one occasion she writes in her journal:

> What I long for is to be able to go out alone! To come and go; to sit down on a bench in the Garden of the Tuileries, or, better still, of the Luxembourg; to stand looking into the artistically arranged shop windows; to visit the churches and museums; to stroll through the old streets of the city in the evening.[53]

Similarly in the case of Gwen John, evidence of her ventures into the public arena – where, indeed, she was invariably approached, propositioned or threatened – does not alter the fact that her choice of the interior was not only a personal preference.

René and John in Paris

Recent work in feminist theory and, especially, lesbian and gay studies has explored the instability of sexual identities and gender identities.[54] This work goes beyond the anti-essentialist argument that gender is a social construct; that femininity and masculinity are categories which vary historically and operate psychically, socially and politically in ways which are both enabling and repressive; and that heterosexuality and homosexuality are relatively recent identities, with their own social-political implications. These constituted identities are now perceived to be fluid and precarious, available at their margins to transgressions which in turn challenge the investment of the dominant culture in absolute boundaries. Female impersonation and cross-dressing, for example, have been seen as important cultural strategies of subversion.[55] Any corporeal, sexual or behavioural practice which registers ambiguity is thus rethought as a radical threat to 'the tyranny of binary sex oppositions'.[56] The focus is primarily on contemporary practices; but a revisionist history of gender also reveals a fascinating array of cases of gender ambiguities, unstable borders and intermediate identities.[57]

Historically, then, this is worth exploring in the case of Paris in the 1900s. The question is whether a social history that understands *flânerie* as gender-based is operating with too 'essentialist' a conception of gender, which does not allow the subtle negotiations available to any men or women who actually inhabited that world. Elizabeth Wilson seems to suggest something like this when she argues that women *could* be *flâneuses*, given the instability of both masculine and feminine identities in the late nineteenth century and the fact that certain women (artists, prostitutes) did have access to the street.[58] Michael Wilson's study of Bohemian Montmartre in the years 1880 to 1910 is more directly relevant to the case of Gwen John (who lived in the other main Parisian artistic community of Montparnasse), and it is a more careful exploration of these questions of gender and social life. The primary transgressive category in the artistic subculture of Montmartre is the woman artist, who assumes the male prerogative of creation; in addition, the active lesbian subculture produced its own gender inversion, in terms of behaviour and dress.[59] So in this context it may be that Rilke and John were relatively exempt from bourgeois codes of appropriate gender behaviour, including access to the street.

In fact, Rilke and John offer themselves as likely candidates for gender transgression in this respect, as the feminized man and the masculinized woman. As is well known, Rilke's mother was disappointed that he was not a girl. She dressed him in girl's clothes until his sixth year and called him Sophie.[60] He was actually christened René, and changed his name to Rainer when he met Lou Andreas-Salomé, who considered his name too feminine.[61] Biddy Martin has argued that the appeal of Rilke to Salomé was his gender ambiguity: 'Rilke seemed both masculine and feminine at once, exemplifying for her the basis of creativity in a primary narcissism and fundamental bisexuality'.[62] In particular, she valued what she saw as his 'feminine' narcissism and receptivity to experience. As I have already suggested, his mode of inhabiting the street was by no means the 'masculine' one of objectivity and distance, but rather an emotional and neurotic experience more appropriate (in gender ideology) to women.

Gwen John, on her side, was not a feminine woman. One writer comments that Rodin favoured a certain masculinity or boyishness in his sitters, and it seems likely that John, as a model, pleased him in the same way.[63] She was often aggressively forward in her romantic and sexual relationships, falling in love with women as much as with men.[64] She was apparently attractive to women, and would sometimes be accosted by women in the street.[65] A certain gender ambiguity is hinted at in the address of her many letters to Rodin, some of which are signed 'John Mary' (Mary was her middle name), and many of which are addressed to an invented figure, 'Julie', though in fact they were intended for Rodin.[66] Nevertheless, despite the unconventional personalities of Rilke and John, and the transgressive possibilities of their milieu in Bohemian Paris in the 1900s, they, and particularly John, were still defined and bound by the social categories of gender in effect at that time.

The discursive city: flâneurs *and* flâneuses

But it is not only the social categories of gender that have been problematized recently. Theoretical developments in urban studies have questioned the sociological assumption that the starting point of the study of space is the existence of physical spatial structures which, though themselves the product of earlier social processes, confront social actors and affect (constrain, determine, allow, facilitate) their actions. With regard to the city itself, James Donald puts the case at its most radical:

> 'The city' does not just refer to a set of buildings in a particular place. To put it polemically, there is no such *thing* as a city. Rather, *the city* designates the space produced by the interaction of historically and geographically specific institutions, social relations of production and reproduction, practices of government, forms and media of communication and so forth... *The city,* then, is above all a representation ... I would argue that the city constitutes an *imagined environment.*[67]

His emphasis is on what the city means in terms of the discourses in which it is conceptualized – medical, social reform, political, surveillance and so on. He contrasts, as an example, the mid-nineteenth-century accounts of Manchester by Engels and by the doctor and reformer James Kay-Shuttleworth, to show how the same physical space can be described quite differently and the sources of its pathology accordingly identified in very different factors. At the level of discourse, then, there is no such thing as the city, as a single, integral, retrievable entity. Stallybrass and White have shown that the social meanings of the nineteenth-century city (the slum and the sewer, for example) were often the projection of psychic fears, expressed in the production of boundaries of area and social class which operated as metaphors for boundaries of the body and its habits.[68] At the level of experience, too, the emphasis has been on the ways in which the inhabitants of the city, or of any public space, negotiate and 'read' that space.[69] The work of Michel de Certeau has been influential in a new sociology of space that focuses on the experiential rather than the social-discursive aspects of the city. He puts the issue like this: 'It is true that the operations of walking on can be traced on city maps in such a way as to transcribe their paths . . . and their trajectories. . . . But these thick or thin curves only refer, like words, to the absence of what has passed by. Surveys of routes miss what was: the act itself of passing by.'[70] The user of a city 'condemns certain places to inertia or disappearance and composes with others spatial "turns of phrase" that are "rare", "accidental" or "illegitimate"'. This he calls a 'rhetoric of walking'.[71]

The phenomenology and semiotics of the city provide a view of urban experience very different from that of structural geographies, which can only perceive the physical conditions of social life – architecture, urban layout, institutions. These approaches also suggest the prospect of limitless possibilities for city users. One conclusion we might therefore draw is that the sociology of separate spheres and the historical observation that women were increasingly excluded from the public arena (including the street) have oversimplified what are in fact the more extensive options for women in the city. The formal accounts, what de Certeau calls the 'conceptual city', will not easily give us access to the ways in which women in the late nineteenth and early twentieth century *were* able to negotiate the streets: the dominant discourses of the city render invisible 'women's city', which a different discourse would entirely re-write. This raises the question of whether the feminist critique of *flânerie* is misplaced. If structural accounts of urban space omit such crucial matters as the way people move through and experience the city, and if it turns out that they are only partial accounts, based on very specific interests and perspectives, could it not be the case that the everyday practices of women were other than those currently visible through the conceptual framework of social histories, namely domestic pursuits, shopping and a kind of nervous scurrying through the streets to protect their respectable status?

The limits of ambiguity: the studio and the street

In this concluding section, I make two claims. First, although 'there is no such thing as a city', the physical structures and social values of urban life still confront denizens of the city, defining the options for their behaviour. Second, while gender identity is a social construct and hence fundamentally unstable, at the centre male and female identities are nevertheless relatively clear. There is no evidence that in Paris in the 1900s women had the opportunity to inhabit the public arena on anything like the same terms as men. Gwen John's 'interior life' has to be understood not just in terms of personal idiosyncrasies, but sociologically, as the particular strategy of existence of a single woman artist in the metropolis.

Social space, including urban space, is of course a social product.[72] It exists as a result of past decisions and practices, situated in particular relations of power and wealth. In that sense, it cannot be conceptualized as the monolithic, unchanging structure in which human interaction takes place. It is also true that in any contemporary present, social actors negotiate the physical and cultural structures of given spatial systems, thereby incrementally transforming them. But it does not follow from this that these structures are phantoms. Henri Lefebvre has shown that we must perceive space as both real and representational. Stressing the symbolic uses of space, he also emphasizes its pre-existent quality:

> Every space is already in place before the appearance in it of actors; these actors are collective as well as individual subjects inasmuch as the individuals are always members of groups or classes seeking to appropriate the space in question. This pre-existence of space conditions the subject's presence, action and discourse, his competence and performance; yet the subject's presence, action and discourse, at the same time as they presuppose this space, also negate it.[73]

Neither the hermeneutics/semiotics of urban life nor the social-historical account of urban transformation should mislead us into thinking that urban structures and associated social (including gender) ideologies are not real. And although we can understand from discourse theory that another account of Paris in 1900 may be possible, mapping the city from the point of view of its traversal by

women, it is still the case that the world of the *flâneur* was a masculine world.

In the same way, recognizing gender ambiguities does not in-
validate social-historical accounts of gender boundaries. On the
contrary, the possibilities of subversion and transgression by gender-
ambiguous practices *depend* on the existence of such boundaries: the
less rigid the boundaries, the less threatening the transgressive act.
In the early years of this century, despite the rise of feminism and
the suffrage movement and the entry of women into some areas of
work and education, the ideology of gender was still strongly in
place. Even in the case of Bohemian Paris, the *femme-artiste* was
unsexed inasmuch as she was perceived as *artist*. As Michael Wilson
says, 'in this unnatural accommodation, one identity must dominate
at the expense of the other'.[74] Women in the lesbian subcultures,
too, encountered a gender inversion which perceived them as 'like
men'. In Bohemian Montmartre, as elsewhere, the gender hierarchy
of men's superiority persists, with gender 'the ground for all their
articulations of identity and difference, no matter how "subversive"
their claims'.[75] In addition, the late nineteenth-century categorization
of women's art as essentially different from that of men was another
obstacle to gender equality in artistic circles.[76]

Gwen John became an artist against the odds. At the Slade School
of Fine Art, she confronted restrictions which male students did not.
Among her female colleagues at the Slade, many of whom won
prizes and top honours, she was one of the few who continued to
devote themselves to their work and the only artist whose reputation
has survived.[77] Her particular circumstances, as exile, artist and
eccentric, provided certain limited possibilities in a world that was
still barely transformed by the changing structures of gender. Within
this space, she was able to create an independent life for herself, as
well as an important series of representations of women who, though
in the private space of the interior, were far from the Victorian
'angel in the house'.[78] But all the evidence shows that there was little
room for manoeuvre in the face of a gender-divided culture. Rilke's
access to the studio and the street, though mediated by his own
neurotic, 'feminine' personality, was still something unavailable to
John. It has been said that for the artist in Paris, 'the studio was part
of the street and the street part of the studio. The relationship was
symbiotic'.[79] For women artists, and for Gwen John, this was not
the case.

NOTES

1 A larger one is in the Musée d'Orsay. For an account of the commission and the history of Rodin's work on the project, see Joy Newton and Margaret MacDonald, 'Rodin: the Whistler Monument', *Gazette des Beaux-Arts*, vol. XCII (December 1978).

2 On John Quinn's support of Gwen John, see Betsy G. Fryberger, 'Gwen John and her patron John Quinn', in *Gwen John: Paintings and Drawings from the Collection of John Quinn and Others* (catalogue, Stanford University Museum of Art, 1982). See also the catalogue of the memorial exhibition of Quinn's collection, *John Quinn 1870–1925. Collection of Paintings, Water Colors, Drawings & Sculpture* (Pidgeon Hill Press, 1926); the catalogue of the sale of the collection, *Paintings and Sculptures: The Renowned Collection of Modern and Ultra-Modern Art Formed by the Late John Quinn* (American Art Association, 1926).

3 Quoted in Michael Holroyd: *Augustus John* (1975), as cited by Cecily Langdale: *Gwen John* (Yale University Press, 1987), p. 2. See also two short essays on his sister by Augustus John: 'Gwendolen John', *The Burlington Magazine*, vol. 81, no. 472 (October 1942); 'Gwen John', in *Chiaroscuro: Autobiography* (Jonathan Cape, 1975 [1952]), pp. 275–84.

4 John, *Chiaroscuro*, p. 277. But Rodin's biographer, Frederic V. Grunfeld, points out that Rodin had no idea 'that Gwen John would one day be regarded as one of the great British painters of the century – and that her drawings would be more avidly collected than his' *Rodin: A Biography* (Henry Holt, 1987), p. 479.

5 Information from a leaflet available in the Salle Camille Claudel, Rodin Museum in Paris (1993). See also ch. 9 of Grunfeld, *Rodin*, and the fictionalized autobiography, *Camille Claudel: Une Femme* by Anne Delbée (Mercury House, 1992).

6 Two exhibitions of her work were important in promoting this reappraisal, at Stanford University Museum of Art in 1982, and at the Barbican Art Gallery, London, and Manchester City Art Gallery in 1985–6. At a recent exhibition and sale of previously unexhibited works in New York, prices of small drawings and watercolours ranged from $2,000 to about $11,000 (Davis & Langdale, 1993).

7 Donald Prater, *A Ringing Glass: The Life of Rainer Maria Rilke* (Clarendon Press, 1986), p. 135.

8 'The model for the head and possibly for the body of the muse was the young English [*sic*] artist, Gwen Mary John, sister of Augustus John. She came to study and work with Rodin in 1905, and later became his mistress. (Her erotic letters to the artist in the Rodin Museum are

signed "Mary John".)' Albert Elsen, *In Rodin's Studio* (Cornell University Press, 1980), p. 185. In fact, Gwen John came to Paris of her own accord, not to study with Rodin. And the date they met, and when she began posing for Rodin, was 1904. Also, she was Welsh. See Langdale, *Gwen John*, p. 31.

9   Ibid., p. 30.

10 David Jenkins, 'Gwen John: an appreciation', in Cecily Langdale and David Fraser Jenkins (eds), *Gwen John: An Interior Life* (Rizzoli, 1985), a catalogue for the exhibition organized by the Barbican Art Gallery in association with the Yale Center for British Art, p. 36.

11 Jenkins, 'Gwen John', p. 40.

12 Langdale, *Gwen John*, p. 33.

13 Grunfeld, *Rodin*, pp. 481, 484, 489, 633. Susan Chitty says that Rodin treated Gwen John distantly, often being rude to her in company: *Gwen John 1876–1939* (Hodder & Stoughton, 1981), pp. 75–6.

14 See my article, 'The invisible *flâneuse*: women and the literature of modernity', *Theory, Culture & Society*, vol. 2, no. 3 (1985), reprinted in *Feminine Sentences: Essays on Women and Culture* (Polity Press, 1990).

15 Belinda Thomson, review, *The Burlington Magazine*, vol. 128, February 1986, p. 163. Richard Cork also stresses her 'reluctan[ce] to move beyond the confines of a studio where she felt relatively secure': 'Gwen John, late Sickert and the Euston Road', in Susan Compton (ed.), *British Art in the 20th Century* (Prestel-Verlag, 1986), p. 246.

16 Langdale and Jenkins, *Gwen John*.

17 Cited in Langdale and Jenkins, *Gwen John*, p. 12.

18 Quoted by Mary Taubman, *Gwen John: The Artist and her Work* (Cornell University Press, 1985), p. 18.

19 1904 at 19 blvd Edgar Quinet; 1906 at 7 rue Saint-Placide; 1907 at 87 rue du Cherche-Midi, which is still standing; 1909 at 6 rue de l'Ouest, which she kept as a studio until 1918, after she moved to Meudon in 1911.

20 Cited by Langdale, *Gwen John*, p. 37. Other commentators point out the continuity in her work with her training (especially in draughtsmanship and in working from the old masters) at the Slade; the influence of Impressionism, as mediated through Whistler, whose school in Paris she had attended in 1898; similarities with the work of the Camden School of artists and members of the New English Art Club in London (Harold Gilman, in particular); the influence of Picasso in his 'blue period'. See, especially, Jenkins, 'Gwen John'; Taubman, *Gwen John*, p. 25; on the Picasso connection, Langdale, *Gwen John*, pp. 37–9; Rotraud Sackerlotzky, 'Gwen John: *Interior: The Brown Teapot*', *Bulletin of the Cleveland Museum of Art*, vol. 75 (April 1988).

21 Chitty, *Gwen John*, p. 97; also pp. 105, 109.
22 On women Impressionists, for example, see Griselda Pollock, 'Modernity and the spaces of femininity', in *Vision and Difference: Femininity, Feminism and Histories of Art* (Routledge, 1988); Kathleen Adler and Tamar Garb: *Berthe Morisot* (Phaidon Press, 1987).
23 A few of her later works, after she moved to Meudon, are of more than one person – people in church, a nun with a group of orphans, a couple walking down a country lane. But even these are not *group* pictures: they do not depict any communication between the people. One such image is of a row of backs of people in church.
24 See Langdale, *Gwen John*; Chitty, *Gwen John*.
25 Thomson, review *The Burlington Magazine*, p. 164; Sackerlotzky, 'Gwen John, *Interior*', p. 109; Jenkins, 'Gwen John', p. 37.
26 Langdale and Jenkins, *Gwen John*, p. 12. In 1908, John wrote to Ursula Tyrwhitt, 'I have met lately a German poet – whom I met some time ago at R[odin]'s – he has lent me a book of love letters of a Portuguese religieuse': cited by Langdale (*Gwen John*, p. 125), who notes that Rilke published an essay on these letters in 1907.
27 John, *Chiaroscuro*, p. 278.
28 Langdale, *Gwen John*, p. 30.
29 Chitty, *Gwen John*, p. 183.
30 Rainer Maria Rilke, *Rodin* (The Fine Editions Press, 1945 [1919]); originally published in 1903.
31 Prater, *A Ringing Glass*.
32 Ibid., p. 132; also *Letters of Rainer Maria Rilke 1892–1910* (W. W. Norton, 1945), p. 209 (letter to Clara).
33 In fact, Rodin did not marry his companion, Rose Beuret, until 1917, two weeks before her death, and ten months before his own, though he had been with her since 1864: Grunfeld, *Rodin*, pp. 633–4, 44. Rilke records, in his account (in a letter to Clara) of his first visit to Rodin, that 'Madame Rodin' was not introduced to him, and that Rodin criticized her for serving the meal late: *Letters*, pp. 80–1.
34 *Letters*, p. 111.
35 Ibid., p. 93.
36 Ibid., p. 281.
37 See, for example, Prater, *A Ringing Glass*, p. 173. However, James Gardner points out important differences between Rilke's own background and that of his invented other self, Malte, 'The mystery of genius', *The New Criterion*, vol. 5, (January 1987). Rilke had originally intended to call this work *The Journal of my Other Self*; see William H. Gass, Introduction to Rilke's *The Notebooks of Malte Laurids Brigge* (Vintage Books, 1985), p. xiv.
38 Rilke, *The Notebooks*, p. 3. Rilke began writing the book in Rome in February 1904 (*Letters*, p. 146), worked on it mostly during 1908

and 1909 and completed it in Leipzig in January 1910 (Prater, *A Ringing Glass*, p. 172).

39   See, for example, Prater, *A Ringing Glass*, p. 98.

40   Naomi Segal, 'Rilke's Paris; "cité pleine de rêves"', in Edward Timms and David Kelley (eds), *Unreal City* (Manchester University Press, 1985).

41   Priscilla Ferguson has suggested that *flânerie* in general had declined by 1879: 'The *flâneur* on and off the streets of Paris', in Keith Tester (ed.), *The Flâneur* (Routledge, 1994).

42   Anne Friedberg, '*Les Flâneurs du Mal(l)*: Cinema and the postmodern condition', *Publications of the Modern Language Association of America*, vol. 106, no. 3 (May 1991), p. 420.

43   Christopher Prendergast, *Paris and the Nineteenth Century* (Blackwell, 1992), p. 34.

44   Naomi Schor, '*Cartes Postales*: representing Paris 1900', *Critical Inquiry*, vol. 18 (Winter 1992), p. 216.

45   Adrian Rifkin, *Street Noises: Parisian Pleasure, 1900–40* (Manchester University Press, 1993), p. 127.

46   Marie Bashkirtseff, *The Journal of a Young Artist 1860–1884* (Cassell, 1889), pp. 195, 417.

47   Cited by Taubman, *Gwen John*, p. 26–7.

48   Chitty, *Gwen John*, pp. 86–9, 76, 118.

49   Ferguson, 'The *flâneur* on and off the streets of Paris'.

50   Rifkin, *Street Noises*, p. 117.

51   'Paris in 1940 had been far from revolutionized. The central city had remained remarkably stable in its physical form, with the most rapid change occurring in the burgeoning residential suburbs following World War One. . . . The period between 1890 and 1940 was characterized by stagnation and impotence.' Norma Evenson, 'Paris, 1890–1940', in Anthony Sutcliffe (ed.), *Metropolis 1890–1940* (Mansell, 1984), p. 282.

52   See my essay, 'The culture of separate spheres: the role of culture in nineteenth-century public and private life', in *Feminine Sentences* (Polity Press, 1990), ch. 2.

53   Bashkirtseff, *The Journal of a Young Artist*, p. 181; also pp. 419–20.

54   See, for example, Judith Butler, *Gender Trouble* (Routledge, 1990) and 'Imitation and gender insubordination', in Diana Fuss (ed.), *Inside/Out: Lesbian Theories, Gay Theories* (Routledge, 1991); Marjorie Garber, *Vested Interests: Cross-Dressing and Cultural Anxiety* (Routledge, 1992); Julia Epstein and Kristina Straub (eds), *Body Guards: The Cultural Politics of Gender Ambiguity* (Routledge, 1991).

55   See Butler, *Gender Trouble*, p. 137: 'In imitating gender, drag implicitly reveals the imitative structure of gender itself.' See also Garber, *Vested Interests*.

56 Epstein and Straub (eds), 'Introduction', *Body Guards*, p. 21.

57 See the essays in Epstein and Straub (eds), *Body Guards*.

58 Elizabeth Wilson, 'The invisible *flâneur*', *New Left Review*, no. 191 (January/February 1992). However, in her concern to resist any suggestion that women were or are passive victims of containment, Wilson overstates the possibilities of resistance for women at that time, slipping from the recognition that the structures of public/private were far from rigid to the argument that masculinity itself was unstable, then to the implication that there was no difference between men and women in their access to the streets and their *flânerie*.

59 Michael Wilson, ' "Sans les femmes, qu'est-ce qui nous resterait": gender and transgression in Bohemian Montmartre', in Epstein and Straub (eds), *Body Guards*, pp. 199, 212.

60 Nora Wydenbruck, *Rilke, Man and Poet* (John Lehmann, 1949), p. 23. In a letter to Ellen Key, written in April 1903, Rilke writes, 'I had to wear very beautiful clothes and went about until school years like a little girl; I believe my mother played with me as with a big doll.' (*Letters*, pp. 98–9.) In his semi-fictional creation, Malte, Rilke describes the boy as his 'Maman's little Sophie . . . whose hair Maman had to braid': *The Notebooks*, p. 99.

61 Wydenbruck, *Rilke*, p. 54. See also Biddy Martin: *Woman and Modernity: The (Life)Styles of Lou Andreas-Salomé* (Cornell University Press, 1991), p. 40.

62 Martin, *Woman and Modernity*, p. 40.

63 Marion J. Hare, 'Rodin and his English sitters', *The Burlington Magazine*, vol. 129 (June 1987), p. 378.

64 Chitty, *Gwen John*, p. 42 (on Grace Westray); p. 61 (on her 'brief passion for a handsome married girl' in Toulouse); p. 69 (on Flodin); p. 182 (on Vera Oumançoff).

65 Ibid., p. 102.

66 Ibid., p. 84.

67 James Donald, 'Metropolis: the city as text', in Robert Bocock and Kenneth Thompson (eds), *Social and Cultural Forms of Modernity* (Polity Press/Open University, 1992), p. 422.

68 Peter Stallybrass and Allon White, *The Politics and Poetics of Transgression* (Methuen, 1986), ch. 3. A detailed, non-psychoanalytic historical example of the social production of the meaning of a city can be found in Robert Darnton's study of Montpellier in 1768: 'A bourgeois puts his world in order: the city as text', in *The Great Cat Massacre and Other Episodes in French Cultural History* (Basic Books, 1984).

69 An early example of such work, more recently taken up again by urban sociologists and geographers, was Kevin Lynch, *The Image of the City* (MIT Press, 1960), which explored the mental image of the city held by its citizens, as they imagine its shape, paths, edges, districts,

landmarks and so on. See also Denis Cosgrove, 'Geography is every-where: culture and symbolism in human landscapes', in Derek Gregory and Rex Walford (eds), *Horizons in Human Geography* (Macmillan, 1989); Denis Cosgrove and Stephen Daniels (eds), *The Iconography of Landscape* (Cambridge University Press, 1988).

70   Michel de Certeau, 'Walking in the city', in *The Practice of Everyday Life* (University of California Press, 1984), p. 97.

71   Ibid., p. 99.

72   See Henri Lefebvre, *The Production of Space* (Basil Blackwell, 1991), p. 26.

73   Ibid., pp. 57, 31–3. See also John Urry's defence of a realist ontology of space, 'Social relations, space and time', in Derek Gregory and John Urry (eds), *Social Relations and Spatial Structures* (Macmillan, 1985); and Elizabeth Grosz's argument for an interactive view of bodies and cities, 'Bodies-cities', in Beatrix Colomina (ed.), *Sexuality and Space* (Princeton Architectural Press, 1992).

74   Wilson, ' "Sans les femmes" ', p. 199.

75   Ibid., p. 217.

76   Tamar Garb, ' "L'art féminin": the formation of a critical category in late nineteenth-century France', *Art History*, vol. 12, no. 1 (March 1989).

77   See Hilary Taylor, ' "If a young painter be not fierce and arrogant God . . . help him": some women artists at the Slade, *c*.1895–9', *Art History*, vol. 9 (June 1986). Taylor suggests (p. 241) that Gwen John's decision to become an artist thrust her into exile and that her exiled existence in France gave her the freedom to pursue this career.

78   See Deborah Cherry and Jane Beckett: 'Gwendolen Mary John (1876–1939)', *Art History*, vol. 11 (September 1988).

79   John Milner, *The Studios of Paris: The Capital of Art in the Late Nineteenth Century* (Yale University Press, 1988), p. 27.

7

On the Road Again: Metaphors of Travel in Cultural Criticism

Theory is a product of displacement, comparison, a certain distance.
To theorize, one leaves home.

James Clifford[1]

A model of political culture appropriate to our own situation will
necessarily have to raise spatial issues as its fundamental organizing
concern. I will therefore provisionally define the aesthetic of such new
(and hypothetical) cultural form as an aesthetic of *cognitive mapping*.

Fredric Jameson[2]

While it is important to recognize the specific power of intellectual
practices, they cannot be separated from our existence as nomadic
subjects in everyday life . . . Cultural critics are co-travelers.

Lawrence Grossberg[3]

Vocabularies of travel seem to have been proliferating in cultural
criticism recently: nomadic criticism, travelling theory, critic-as-tourist
and vice versa, maps, billboards, hotels and motels. There are good
reasons why these particular metaphors are in play in current critical
thought, and I shall review some later. Mainly, I want to suggest that
these metaphors are *gendered*, in a way that is for the most part not
acknowledged. That is they come to critical discourse encumbered
with a range of gender connotations which, I will argue, have implications for what we do with them in cultural studies. My argument
is that just as the practices and ideologies of *actual* travel operate to
exclude or pathologize women, so the use of that vocabulary as

metaphor necessarily produces androcentric tendencies *in theory*. It will not do, therefore, to modify this vocabulary in the attempt to take account of women, as some critics have suggested we might do. Some discourses are too heavily compromised by the history of their usage, and it may be that the discourse of travel, or at least certain discourses of travel, should be understood in this way.

Gender is not, of course, the only dimension involved in travel. Disparities of wealth and cultural capital, and class difference generally, have always ensured real disparities in access to and modes of travel. In addition, it is clear that the *ways* in which people travel are very diverse, ranging from tourism, exploring and other voluntary activity to the forced mobility of immigrant and guest workers in many countries, and to the extremes of political and economic exile. In examining here a single notion of travel, which for the most part rests on a Western, middle-class idea of the chosen and leisured journey, I am merely taking as my subject that metaphor which is in play in these particular discourses. (That this idea of travel operates here is another important question deserving examination, but it is not my focus here.)

Theory and travel

Quite apart from the increasing use of travel metaphors in critical theory, a number of cultural analysts have been writing about travel itself.[4] Dean MacCannell's *The Tourist*, first published in 1976, was reissued in 1989 with a new introduction in which the author responds to more recent work on theory and travel.[5] Other studies of travel include John Urry's *The Tourist Gaze*, and essays on the semiotics of travel by Jonathan Culler and John Frow.[6] The work of travel writers is also more prominent, with (at least on an impressionistic rather than statistical count) more review space in newspapers and journals.[7] In some cases, the work of travel writers is cited by theorists of travel and travel-theory, as for example in James Clifford's reference to Bruce Chatwin.[8] Clearly this is a restless moment in cultural history.

In MacCannell's account of the nature of tourism, we are first presented with the idea that the tourist is typical of the modern person and, in particular, of the social theorist. In all three cases, it is a question of reacting to the increased differentiation of the contemporary world and the consequent loss of sense or meaning. 'Sightseeing is a kind of collective striving for a transcendence of the modern totality, a way of attempting to overcome the discontinuity of modernity, of incorporating its fragments into unified experience.'[9] Social and cultural theory are then reconceptualized as a kind of tourism, or sightseeing, founded on the search for authenticity and the attempt to make sense of the social. (In the introduction to the second edition of the book, however, MacCannell firmly distances himself from post-modern theories which take the more radical view that there is no social, or that there is no fundamental, 'real' structure below the play of signifiers. In this respect his notion of sightseeing is something like Jameson's concept of 'mapping', which is also based on the need to negotiate the lost, but still existing, totality.)

A different link between travel and theory is made in Edward Said's influential essay, 'Traveling theory'.[10] Somewhat strangely, the use made of the notion of this theory has not always had much to do with Said's argument in that piece, in which he is interested in the question of what happens to theory when it does travel – for example, the transformations of a theory in passing from Lukàcs to Goldmann to Raymond Williams, and its location and interpretation in very different historical and political moments. (Said also refers to this as 'borrowed' theory.) This is not the same thing as arguing that there is something mobile in the *nature* of theory, which is the way the notion of 'travelling theory' has been interpreted. In other words, the fact that theories sometimes travel and mutate does not mean that theory, transported or not, is essentially itinerant. Actually, both senses of 'travelling theory' are in currency in cultural criticism.

Post-colonial criticism and travel

The first quotation in this chapter, from James Clifford, has to be seen in the context of important developments in post-colonial criticism. Here, the metaphors of mobility operate to destabilize the fixed and ethnocentric categories of traditional anthropology. Clifford is one of many cultural theorists who have recently revolutionized the methodologies and conceptual frameworks of cross-cultural study, at the same time demonstrating and deconstructing the entrenched ideologies of self and other on which such study has been based. For him the metaphor of 'travel' helps to de-essentialize both researcher and subject of research and begins to transform the unacknowledged relationship of power and control which characterized post-colonial encounters. Here, the notion of 'travel' operates in two ways. It is both literal – the ethnographer *does* leave home to do research – and epistemological – it describes knowledge in a different way, as contingent and partial. Related 'travel' vocabulary in this particular discourse includes Clifford's invocation of the hotel as 'a site of travel encounters', rather than either a fixed residence or a tent in a village.[11] It is a notion (or, as he puts it, following Bakhtin, a 'chronotope') that registers both location and its provisional nature.

Post-modern theory and the need for maps

The second quotation is from Fredric Jameson's important essay on post-modernism as 'the cultural logic of late capitalism'.[12] The motivation behind a travel vocabulary here and in the next case I shall take has something in common with its location in post-colonial criticism: that is the response to and attempt to negotiate a crisis in both the social and the representational in the late twentieth century. Nevertheless, we should not equate post-coloniality, post-modern theory and post-structuralism, though it is important to keep in mind that there are intellectual and political links between them.

Jameson's notion of 'cognitive mapping' (spelled out in more detail in a subsequent essay[13]) is offered as a metaphor that captures the nature of theory in the post-modern age. As is well known, Jameson's argument here is that in the era of late capitalism it is no longer possible to perceive the social totality. At the level of the economy, multinational capitalism is not visible in the way that entrepreneurial capitalism, and even monopoly capitalism, were. At the level of technology, steam and electric power (characterizing respectively the two earlier stages of capitalism) have given way to the hidden processes of nuclear power and electronic knowledge. The social subject, and *a fortiori* the sociologist and cultural critic, must therefore resort to new strategies of orientation and analysis. Already immersed in the chaotic and disorganized flow of late capitalist society, the only strategy is to 'map' the social from within. Like MacCannell (and unlike other theorists of the post-modern) Jameson has not given up on totality himself. His argument is that we need new ways of grasping and understanding the fundamental social structures and processes in which we live.[14]

Post-structuralism and nomadic subjects

The third theoretical origin of travel vocabularies, and the last I shall discuss here, is the post-structuralist theory of the subject. The product of radical semiotics, Lacanian psychoanalytic theory and deconstruction, this critique demonstrates the fluid and provisional nature of the subject, which must now be seen as de-centred. In the context of media studies and reception theory, Gilles Deleuze's notion of the 'nomadic subject' has been found to be a useful way to acknowledge the television viewer's or the reader's complex ability to engage with a text both from a position of identity and in an encounter which also potentially *changes* that identity. Lawrence Grossberg puts it like this: 'The nomadic subject is amoeba-like, struggling to win some space for itself in its local context. While its shape is always determined by its nomadic articulations, it always has a shape which is itself effective.'[15] Similarly, Janice Radway has employed the notion of the nomadic subject to provide the necessary conception of readers and viewers as active producers of meaning in their engagement with texts.[16]

Related metaphors of travel here are the idea of 'billboards' as signposts that 'do not tell us where we are going but merely announce . . . the town we are passing through'[17] and the concept of the 'commuter', also suggested by Grossberg.[18]

Off the road: women and travel

So far, I have located the emergence of vocabularies of travel in three related major theoretical developments: post-colonial criticism, post-modern theory and post-structuralist theories of the subject. There is no doubt that in each case the metaphors have proved useful and suggestive and promise specific solutions to the ideological effects of dominant terminologies. In all three cases, it is easy to see why notions of mobility, fluidity, provisionality and process have been preferable to alternative notions of stasis and fixity. In cultural criticism in the late twentieth century we have had to realize that only ideologies and vested interests 'fix' meaning, and it is the job of cultural critics to destabilize those meanings.

This work has already been criticized on a number of counts. The radical relativism of some of these texts has proved unacceptable for those who are not prepared to abandon certain metanarratives. There is also a tension between what we might think of as the more and less radical versions of semiotics: in short, it is a question of what, if anything, lies behind the play of signifiers in our culture. From the point of view of engaged politics, and here specifically in relation to feminism, a certain post-modern stance is incompatible with the fundamental commitment to a critique which is premised on the existence of systematically structured, actual inequalities, including those of gender. In a recent critique of some tendencies in cultural studies in the United States, the point is made in this way: 'Unless it is reflexive and critical, nomadic subjectivity is unlikely to organize meaningful political thought or activity, especially against elites whose thinking is more organized and purposeful. People who are nomads cannot settle down.'[19]

I do not wish to rehearse the various critiques of 'post' theories here, but instead to focus on the narrower case of a possible feminist critique of travel metaphors.

The *un*theoretical and coincidental origin of my unease with this vocabulary was twofold. Like many other people, I had read Bruce Chatwin's *The Songlines*[20] when it first came out. Also like many of its readers, I found it a compelling journal of the author's travels in Australia. At the same time I felt, in a somewhat unarticulated way, alienated from it as a 'masculine' text. In particular, in a long section of the book consisting entirely of quotations about travel (including some from Chatwin's own diaries from other travels), I had the sense that women did not travel like this.[21] The fact that Clifford and others cite this particular text mobilized that reaction again.

Secondly, I had been doing some work on the 1950s, specifically on the fantasy of 'America' in Britain in that decade.[22] In this connection, I was reading newly published accounts of the period by the women of the beat generation: Joyce Johnson, Carolyn Cassady, Hettie Jones. This was the other side of the stories we already knew, a side until now unrecorded: as the title of Cassady's book puts it, what it was like 'off the road'. Reading Johnson (one of Kerouac's women) and Cassady together was illuminating – one woman on each coast, both waiting for Jack or Neal (in Cassady's case sometimes for both) to get back. Johnson once wondered if she could join Kerouac *on* the road.

> In 1957, Jack was still traveling on the basis of pure, naive faith that always seemed to renew itself for his next embarkation despite any previous disappointments. He would leave me very soon and go to Tangier . . . I'd listen to him with delight and pain, seeing all the pictures he painted so well for me, wanting to go with him. Could he ever include a woman in his journeys? I didn't altogether see why not. Whenever I tried to raise the question, he'd stop me by saying that what I really wanted were babies. That was what all women wanted and what I wanted too, even though I said didn't . . . I said of course I wanted babies someday, but not for a long time, not now. Wisely, sadly, Jack shook his head.[23]

Reading these texts, I was already sensitized to certain questions of gender and travel, and perhaps suspicious of the appearance of travel metaphors in cultural theory. But this, of course, only raises the question of whether such metaphors are gendered – it does not decide the issue.[24]

Histories of travel make it clear that women have never had the same access to the road as men.

> In many societies being feminine has been defined as sticking close to home. Masculinity, by contrast, has been the passport for travel. Feminist geographers and ethnographers have been amassing evidence revealing that a principal difference between women and men in countless societies has been the licence to travel away from a place thought of as 'home'.[25]

In a major study of travel over centuries, Eric Leed makes similar generalizations about gender imbalances.

> The erotics of arrival are predicated on certain realities in the history of travel: the sessility of women; the mobility of men . . . In the conditions of settlement and civility, travel is 'genderized' and becomes a 'gendering' activity. Historically, men have traveled and women have not, or have traveled only under the aegis of men, an arrangement that has defined the sexual relations in arrivals as the absorption of the stranger – often young, often male – within a nativizing female ground.[26]

Of course, women do have a place in travel, as also in tourism. Often that place is marginal and degraded. John Urry and Cynthia Enloe both discover women in the tourist industry in the role of hotel maids, or active in sex-tourism.[27] For the most part women have generally had a limited access and a problematic relation to varieties of travel.[28]

However, it is not simply that travel is predominantly what men do. It may be, too, that there is something *intrinsically* masculine about travel, and that therefore using travel metaphors has serious implications. At this point, however, I should note that at least two cultural critics recognize that there is a problem. Clifford acknowledges that travel and, therefore, travel metaphors are not gender-neutral.

> The marking of 'travel' by gender, class, race, and culture is all too clear . . . . 'Good travel' (heroic, educational, scientific, adventurous, ennobling) is something men (should) do. Women are impeded from serious travel.[29]

Meaghan Morris, who has also employed travel metaphors in her recent work, makes the same point.

> But, of course, there is a very powerful cultural link – one particularly dear to a masculinist tradition inscribing 'home' as the site both of frustrating containment (home as dull) and of truth to be rediscovered (home as real). The stifling home is the place from which the voyage begins and to which, in the end, it returns . . . The tourist leaving and returning to the blank space of the *domus* is, and will remain, a sexually in-different 'him'.[30]

Her suggestion is that the metaphor of the 'motel' may prove more appropriate for a non-androcentric cultural theory.

> With its peculiar function as a place of escape yet as a home-away-from-home, the motel can be rewritten as a transit-place for women able to use it . . . Motels have had liberating effects in the history of women's mobility.[31]

The question is: What is the link between women's exclusion from travel and uses of notions of travel in cultural theory and analysis? And then: Will modified metaphors of travel avoid the risk of androcentrism in theory?

Masculininity and travel

If it is only a *contingent* fact that, as Leed says, 'historically, men
have traveled and women have not', there may be no reason to
argue that the vocabulary of travel is irrevocably compromised and,
hence, unacceptable in cultural criticism. However, it is possible that
the connection is not just contingent, but that there is an *intrinsic*
relationship between masculinity and travel. By 'intrinsic' I do not
mean 'essential'; rather my interest is in the centrality of travel/
mobility to *constructed* masculine identity. Leed himself has a fairly
straightforward view of what he calls the 'spermatic journey'. He
argues that it is likely that 'much travel is stimulated by a male
reproductive motive, a search for temporal extensions of self in
children, only achievable through the agency of women'.[32] In this
view, women's identification with place is the result of reproductive
necessities that require stability and protection by men.[33] Such an
account, however, does not help us to explain the persistence of
these arrangements in totally transformed circumstances.

Mary Gordon has argued that men's journeys should be construed
as flight from women. In an essay on American fiction, she notes the
centrality of the image of motion connected with the American hero;
authors she discusses include Faulkner, Dreiser and Updike. At work
here is 'a habit of association that connects females with stasis and
death; males with movement and life'.[34] Indeed, she notes how frequently in such fiction a female has to be killed to ensure the man's
escape. According to her, 'the woman is the centripetal force pulling
[the hero] not only from natural happiness but from heroism as
well'.[35] I think it would be possible to pursue this suggestion in
psychoanalytic terms: for example, feminists have used the very different work of Nancy Chodorow and Julia Kristeva to explore the
male investment in strong ego boundaries and the consequent and
continuing fear of engulfment in the female and loss of self.

In MacCannell's account of tourism, the search for 'authenticity'
is foregrounded. By this he means the attempt to overcome the sense
of fragmentation and to achieve a 'unified experience', which is less
to do with the 'authentic' *self* than to do with a quest for an authentic *social* meaning. But tourism and sightseeing can be seen just as
much to operate as productive for the post-modern self so frequently
diagnosed by sociologists, and to that extent the gender implications

are equally clear – if, that is, we do take the view that in our culture men have a different and exaggerated investment in a concept of a 'self'. Some years ago, two British sociologists wrote a book whose subtitle is 'The theory and practice of resistance to everyday life'.[36] I wondered why one would need to *resist* everyday life, by which the authors mainly mean routine, meaninglessness, the domestic, repetitiveness. Certainly the particular account they give, both of that everyday life and of the types and strategies of resistance discussed (including fantasy, hobbies, role-distance, holidays) are, to say the least, extraordinarily *male*. Could such a text be written from the point of view of women, or in a gender-neutral way? Probably not.

My suggestion that a connection between masculinity, travel and self can be made is not unproblematic. First, I could argue the opposite case, based on the same theories. For example, since (according to Chodorow and others) women are produced as gendered subjects at the expense of any clear sense of self, of definite ego boundaries – the result of inadequate separation from the mother – one might think that women have *more* of an investment in discovering a self and that, if travel is a mode of discovery, then that this would have a strong attraction to women. Indeed, Dea Birkett, in her study of Victorian lady travellers, has suggested that it operated this way for some women, whose fragile sense of identity collapsed on the death of parents in relation to whom they defined themselves.[37] Here I think the important distinction is between the defence of a precarious but already constructed self (the masculine identity) and an unformed sense of self, but one less crucial to identity. The investment in travel in relation to the former seems to me potentially far greater.

Secondly, the notion of feminine identity as relational, fluid, without clear boundaries seems more congruent with the perpetual mobility of travel than is the presumed solidity and objectivity of masculine identity. And thirdly, and related to this, it could be argued that women have an interest in destabilizing what is fixed in a patriarchal culture, as those who propose an alliance between feminism and post-modernism have suggested, and hence that methods and tactics of movement, including travel, seem appropriate.[38] I shall return to these last two points later to suggest that such destabilizing has to be from *a location*, and that simple metaphors of unrestrained mobility are both risky and inappropriate.

I have not analysed in depth the gendered nature of travel and escape, but have indicated some of the ways in which this might be pursued. This chapter explores how metaphors of travel work. So far, I hope to have shown that they are, in fact and perhaps in essence, androcentric. For although it is interesting to pursue the possible connection between masculinity and travel, my real interest is in the discursive construction involved, in the ways narratives of travel, which are in play in the metaphoric use of the vocabulary, are gendered. As Georges Van Den Abbeele has argued, although there is nothing exclusively masculine about travel, in the sense that women have certainly travelled, nevertheless 'Western ideas about travel and the concomitant corpus of voyage literature have generally – if not characteristically – transmitted, inculcated, and reinforced patriarchal values and ideology'.[39] The discourse of travel, he suggests, typically functions as a 'technology of gender'.

Women who travel

The main objection to my argument so far is that, in fact, women *do* travel.[40] The case of the Victorian lady travellers is the prime example.[41] Isabella Bird, Isabelle Eberhardt, Mary Kingsley, Freya Stark, Marianne North, Edith Durham and many other redoubtable women at the end of the nineteenth century and beginning of the twentieth left homes that were often extremely constraining in order to travel the world in the most difficult and challenging circumstances. Their lives and their journeys have been well documented, both by themselves and by subsequent historians.[42] If indeed travel is gendered as male and women's travel restricted here is a case when, at a moment of exaggerated gender ideologies of women's domestic mission, the most dramatic exceptions occur. It is interesting, here, to consider how this travel was construed and constructed, both by the travellers themselves and by the cultures they left and returned to.

Dea Birkett has suggested that in an important way these women inhabited the position of men. In fact, they rarely dressed as men (Hester Stanhope and Isabelle Eberhardt were among the few who did) though they did, like Isabella Bird, sometimes modify their dress in a practical way. Nor did they define themselves as anything other than feminine (and in many cases, also anti-feminist). But the relationship of authority they unquestioningly established with the natives of places they visited and traversed (they were often addressed as 'Sir'[43]), overrode considerations of gender. 'As women travellers frequently pointed to the continuities and similarities with earlier European male travellers, the supremacy of distinctions of race above those of sex allowed them to take little account of their one obvious difference from these forbears – the fact they were female.'[44] Birkett also suggests that many of the women travellers had a strong identifification with their fathers from an early age, and through that identification learned to value the prospect of escape and freedom, since several, Ella Christie and Mary Kingsley for example, had fathers who travelled widely. 'Their mothers', and sometimes sisters', domestic spheres were associated with cloistered, cramped ambition and human suffering. In response, they created their own sense of stability and belonging in exploring their paternal ancestors, thereby reinforcing their identity with their father and his lineage.'[45] Bird resolved some of the problems of gender-identification which 'masculine' travel could have produced by externalizing the feminine in her sister Henrietta, to the extent that on Henrietta's death in 1880 she 'lost her ability to revel with impunity in her travels',[46] and in fact married at 50 and settled for a while back in Scotland. Sisters played a similar role, as conscience, home-self, and recipient of journal-letters, in the travels of Ella Christie, Mary Slessor and Agnes Smith Lewis. This suggestion of the coexistence of two identifications is attested to by Bird's remarkably dual life. She started travelling in her forties, having till then lived the life of the frail and sometimes invalid daughter of a Victorian clergyman. She travelled to Hawaii, to Australia, across the Rockies on horseback, to India, Persia, Korea, China and, at the age of 70, Morocco. Between travels, back in England and Scotland, she invariably became ill again and spent much of the time on her day bed.

When women do travel, then, their *mode* of negotiating the road is crucial. The responses to the lady travellers of those back home are also illuminating in their own contradictory negotiation of a threatening anomaly. Birkett discusses the reactions of the press, other travellers and members of the Royal Geographical Society; these included minimizing the travels (in comparison with those undertaken by male explorers), stressing the femininity of these women (despite such masculine pursuits) and hinting that their conduct overseas might well have been improper. In other words, we do not need to discover that women travellers were in any straightforward sense 'masculine' to conclude that their activities positioned them in important ways as at least problematic with regard to gender identification.[47]

The gendering of travel is not premised on any simple notion of public and private spheres – a categorization that feminist historians have shown was in any case more an ideology of place than the reality of the social world. What is in operation here *is* that ideology. The ideological construction of 'woman's place' works to render invisible, problematic and, in some cases impossible, women 'out of place'. Lesley Harman, in her study of homeless women in Toronto, shows how the myth of home constructs homeless women and homeless men in very different ways. As she puts it, 'the very notion of "homelessness" among women cannot be invoked without noting the ideological climate in which this condition is framed as problematic, in which the deviant categories of "homeless woman" and "bag lady" are culturally produced'.[48] It is not entirely frivolous to consider the hysterical and violent responses to the film *Thelma and Louise* in the same way. As Janet Maslin has pointed out, the activities of this travelling duo are as nothing compared with the destruction wrought in many male road movies.[49] She writes in response to an unprecedented barrage of hostile reviews, for example:

> Any movie that went as far out of its way to trash women as this female chauvinist sow of a film does to trash men would be universally, and justifiably, condemned . . . The movie portrays Sarandon and Davis as sympathetic. . . . The music and the banter suggest a couple of good ole gals on a lark; the content suggests two self-absorbed, irresponsible, worthless people.[50]

The ideological gendering of travel as male both impedes female travel and renders problematic the self-definition of and response to women who *do* travel. I do not claim to have offered an analysis of this gendering, though I have suggested that, for example, a psychoanalytic account would be worth pursuing. Nor, once again, am I arguing that women *don't* travel. I am primarily interested in seeing how *metaphors and ideologies of travel* operate. In the final section, I shall consider the implications of this for a cultural theory which relies on such metaphors.

Feminism, travel and place

Many feminists have made the point about post-structuralist theory that just as women are discovering their subjectivity and identity, theory tells us that we have to deconstruct and de-centre the subject. Susan Bordo has identified the somewhat suspicious timing by which 'gender' evaporates into 'genders' at the moment women gain some power in critical discourse and academic institutions.[51] In the same way, just as women accede to theory, male theorists take to the road. Without claiming any conspiracy or even intention, we can see what are, in my view, exclusionary moves in the academy. The already gendered language of mobility marginalizes women who want to participate in cultural criticism. For that reason, there is no point in tinkering with the vocabulary of travel (motels instead of hotels) to accommodate women. Crucially, this is still the wrong language.

How is it that metaphors of movement and mobility, often invoked in the context of radical projects of destabilizing discourses of power, can have conservative effects? It might seem that feminism, like post-colonial criticism, can only benefit from participating in a critique of stasis. Here we confront the same paradox as in the proposed alliance between feminism and post-modernism. The appeal of post-modernism lies in its demolition of grand narratives, narratives which have silenced women and minorities. The problem with an over-enthusiastic embrace of the post-modern is that that same critique undermines the very basis of feminism, itself necessarily a particular narrative. Feminists have only reached provisional conclusions here, based on either a relative rejection of grand narratives or a pragmatic retention of less grand theory.

In the same way, destabilizing has to be *situated*, if the critic is not to self-destruct in the process. The problem with terms like 'nomad', 'maps' and 'travel' is that they are not usually located; hence (and purposely) they suggest ungrounded and unbounded movement, since the whole point is to resist fixed selves/viewers/subjects. But the consequent suggestion of free and equal mobility is itself a deception, since we do not all have the same access to the road. Women's critique of the static, the dominant, has to make two important acknowledgements: first, that what is to be criticized is, to retain the geographic metaphor, the *dominant centre*; secondly, that the criticism (the destabilizing tactics) originates from a place too – the margins, the edges, the less visible spaces. There are other metaphors of space that I find very suggestive, and which may be less problematic, at least in this respect: 'borderlands', 'exile', 'margins': all are premised on the fact of dislocation from a given, excluding place. Elspeth Probyn recommends we start from the body – what Adrienne Rich has called 'the politics of location' – to insist on the situated nature of experience and political critique.[52] Caren Kaplan's use of the notion of 'deterritorialization' similarly assumes a territory from which one is displaced and which one negotiates, dismantles, perhaps returns to.[53]

For all these metaphors there is a centre. In a patriarchal culture we are not all, as cultural critics any more than social beings, 'on the road' together. We therefore have to think carefully about employing a vocabulary that, liberating in many ways, also encourages the irresponsibility of flight and misleadingly implies a notion of universal and equal mobility. This involves challenging the exclusions of a metaphoric discourse of travel.

Metaphors, however, are not static.[54] My critique of the specific metaphors of travel in relation to gender should not, therefore, be read as either a ban on metaphors (which are inevitable in thought and writing and which always import certain limits and ideologies) or as a definitive condemnation of travel metaphors, but rather as a provisional and situated analysis of the current working of discourse. In the end, too, a different critical strategy might be the *reappropriation*, not the avoidance, of such metaphors – a good post-modern practice, which both exposes the implicit meanings in play and produces the possibility of subverting those meanings in the context of a different discourse.

NOTES

1 James Clifford, 'Notes on travel and theory', *Inscriptions*, no. 5 (1989), p. 177.
2 Fredric Jameson, 'Postmodernism, or the cultural logic of late capitalism', *New Left Review*, no. 146 (1984), p. 89.
3 Lawrence Grossberg, 'Wandering audiences, nomadic critics', *Cultural Studies*, vol. 2, no. 3 (1988), pp. 388–9.
4 In David Lodge's latest novel, *Paradise News* (Viking, 1992), a professor investigates the sightseeing tour as secular pilgrimage.

5 Dean MacCannell, *The Tourist: A New Theory of the Leisure Class* (Schocken Books: 1989 [1976]). An early example of the current interest in travel and theory, however, was Georges Van Den Abbeele's review of MacCannell's book, four years after its publication: 'Sightseers: the tourist as theorist', *Diacritics*, December 1980.

6 John Urry, *The Tourist Gaze: Leisure and Travel in Contemporary Society* (Sage, 1990); Jonathan Culler, 'The semiotics of tourism', in *Framing the Sign: Criticism and its Institutions* (University of Oklahoma Press, 1988) – the essay originally published in 1981; John Frow, 'Tourism and the semiotics of nostalgia', *October*, no. 57, (1991).

7 For example, the full-length, front-page symposium in *The New York Times Book Review*, 18 August 1991, entitled 'Itchy feet and pencils', in which Jan Morris, Russell Banks, Robert Stone and William Styron discuss travel writing.

8 Clifford, 'Notes on travel and theory', p. 183.

9 MacCannell, *The Tourist*, p. 13.

10 Edward W. Said, 'Traveling theory', in *The World, the Text, and the Critic* (Harvard University Press, 1983).

11 James Clifford, 'Travelling cultures', in Lawrence Grossberg, Cary Nelson and Paula Treichler (eds), *Cultural Studies* (Routledge, 1992), p. 101.

12 Jameson, 'Postmodernism'.

13 Fredric Jameson, 'Cognitive mapping', in Cary Nelson and Lawrence Grossberg (eds), *Marxism and the Interpretation of Culture* (Macmillan, 1988).

14 In a different use of the metaphor of a 'map', Iain Chambers, describing the intellectual as a 'humble detective', explicitly abandons the idea of social totality: 'Maps for the metropolis: a possible guide to the present', *Cultural Studies*, vol. 1, no. 1 (1987).

15 Lawrence Grossberg, 'The in-difference of television', *Screen*, vol. 28, no. 2 (1987), p. 39. See also his essays, 'Experience, signification, and reality: the boundaries of cultural semiotics', *Semiotica* 41–1/4, and 'Wandering audiences, nomadic critics'.

16 Janice Radway, 'Reception study: ethnography and the problems of dispersed audiences and nomadic subjects', *Cultural Studies*, vol. 2, no. 3 (1988). See also Meaghan Morris: 'At Henry Parkes Motel', *Cultural Studies*, vol. 2, no. 1 (1988). My knowledge of Deleuze's work is mostly secondary, but in his essay 'Nomad thought' Deleuze means something rather different: the nomad as someone who opposes centralized power: in David Allison (ed.), *The New Nietzsche* (Delta, 1977), pp. 148–9. This seems to have nothing to do with the decentred subject, but more with the idea of displaced (groups of) people, able to contest authority from the outside.

17 Grossberg, 'The in-difference of television', p. 31; Morris, 'At Henry Parkes Motel'.

18 Grossberg, 'Wandering audiences', p. 384. This metaphor does not work so well, I think. Grossberg says 'Nomadic subjects are like "commuters" moving between different sites of daily life. . . . Like commuters, they are constantly shaped by their travels, by the roads they traverse. . . . And like commuters, they take many different kinds of trips, beginning from different starting-points, punctuated by different interruptions and detours, and arriving at different stopping-points.' But surely the central characteristic of commuting is that you always start from the *same* starting-point and end at the *same* stopping-point: primarily, of course, home and work-place.

19 Mike Budd, Robert M. Entman and Clay Steinman, 'The affirmative character of US cultural studies', *Critical Studies in Mass Communication*, vol. 7 (1990), p. 176.

20 Bruce Chatwin, *The Songlines* (Penguin, 1987).

21 When I went back to read that section, some forty pages of text, quotation, and aphorism, I could not find very much to support my sense of it as 'masculine'. It even included a reference to nomadic cultures in which it is the women who initiate the move. One entry was clearly 'male', even misogynistic:

> To the Arabian bedouin, Hell is a sunlit sky and the sun a strong, bony female – mean, old and jealous of life – who shrivels the pastures and the skin of humans. The moon, by contrast, is a lithe and energetic young man, who guards the nomad while he sleeps, guides him on night journeys, brings rain and distils the dew on plants. He has the misfortune to be married to the sun. He grows thin and wasted after a single night with her. It takes him a month to recover. (Chatwin, *The Songlines*, p. 201.)

Nevertheless, I retained the feeling that I was 'reading as a man' here, a feeling which partly motivated the initial attempt in this chapter to analyse that feeling.

22 See the final chapter in this book – 'Angry Young Men and Minor (Female) Characters'.

23 Joyce Johnson, *Minor Characters* (Picador, 1983), p. 126. This is also cited by Alix Kates Shulman in her review of *Minor Characters*: 'The Beat Queens: Boho chicks stand by their men', *Voice Literary Supplement*, June 1989. See also Carolyn Cassady: *Off the Road: My Years with Cassady, Kerouac, and Ginsberg* (Wm Morrow, 1990).

24 For one thing, it may be that the 1950s, and more particularly the so-called Beat Generation, constituted a very specific phenomenon, in

which case any generalization would be totally misconceived. It is part of my project here to examine how general the gendering of travel may be. But here I could also mention a recent piece of journalism, which replays Kerouac/Cassady, if in ironic form. Nicolas Cage, the movie actor, wrote a piece for the magazine *Details*, July 1991, entitled 'On the road, again: retracing Kerouac's footsteps in the wild heart of the country', documenting his drive from Los Angeles to New Orleans and his experiences and reflections en route. To me, both the events and the recollections seem very much in the Kerouac mode, despite a certain self-awareness and irony (for example, in relating the fact that the first car he took broke down when he and his friend were 'still comfortably within the 213 area code').

25 Cynthia Enloe, *Bananas, Beaches and Bases: Making Feminist Sense of International Politics* (University of California Press, 1989), p. 21.

26 Eric J. Leed, *The Mind of the Traveller: From Gilgamesh to Global Tourism* (Basic Books, 1991), p. 113.

27 Urry, *The Tourist Gaze*; Enloe, *Bananas, Beaches and Bases*.

28 Another example, from Judith Adler's history of tramping, also confirms the tendency for such undirected mobility to be the preserve of men: 'Youth on the road: reflections on the history of tramping', *Annals of Tourism Research*, vol. 12 (1985).

29 Clifford, 'Travelling cultures', p. 105.

30 Morris, 'At Henry Parkes Motel', p. 12.

31 Ibid., p. 2.

32 Leed, *The Mind of the Traveller*, p. 114.

33 This is an argument that was used, a few years ago, by feminist anthropologists concerned to explain the historical and apparently universal oppression and domestication of women. Here, as in its other manifestations, it is an argument that raises as many problems as it solves.

34 Mary Gordon, 'Good boys and dead girls', in *Good Boys and Dead Girls and Other Essays* (Viking, 1991), p. 17.

35 Ibid., p. 6.

36 Stanley Cohen and Laurie Taylor: *Escape Attempts: The Theory and Practice of Resistance to Everyday Life* (Allen Lane, 1976; new edition, Routledge, 1992).

37 Dea Birkett, *Spinsters Abroad: Victorian Lady Explorers* (Victor Gollancz, 1991), p. 71. This is an issue I also take up in ch. 1, 'The Female Stranger'.

38 Here Deleuze's sense of 'nomad criticism', mentioned in n. 16 above, is more appropriate than the usage I have taken up in this chapter.

39 Georges Van Den Abbeele, *Travel as Metaphor: From Montaigne to Rousseau* (University of Minnesota Press, 1992), pp. xxv–xxvi.

40 Often, the fact of women's travels has been obscured by historians and other narrators. As Gordon DesBrisay has pointed out to me, recent historical research has shown that in early modern Scotland women were more mobile than has generally been thought. See Ian D. Whyte, 'The geographical mobility of women in early modern Scotland', in Leah Leneman (ed.), *Perspectives in Social History: Essays in Honour of Rosalind Mitchison* (Aberdeen University Press, 1988).

41 I could, of course, have taken other examples – contemporary women explorers, round-the-world yachtswomen, female truckers, for instance. Many of the suggestions I make here about the Victorians would then probably be seen as specific to their case.

42 Birkett, *Spinsters Abroad*; Isabelle Eberhardt: *The Passionate Nomad: The Diary of Isabelle Eberhardt* (Virago, 1987); Dorothy Middleton: *Victorian Lady Travellers* (Academy Chicago, 1965); Mary Russell: *The Blessings of a Good Thick Skirt: Women Travellers and their World* (Collins, 1988).

43 Birkett, *Spinsters Abroad*, p. 117.

44 Ibid., p. 125.

45 Ibid., p. 18.

46 Ibid., p. 95.

47 Box Car Bertha, who spent her life on the road, took advantage of similar ambiguities in gender identification, in this case in her unusual upbringing.

> My childhood was completely free and always mixed up with the men and women on the road. There weren't many dolls or toys in my life but plenty of excitement. . . . We took for playthings all the grand miscellany to be found in a railroad yard. We built houses of railroad ties so big that it took four of us to lift one of them in place. We invented games that made us walk the tracks . . . We played with the men's shovels and picks and learned to use them . . . We girls dressed just like the boys, mostly in hand-me-down overalls. No one paid much attention to us. (In Lisa St Aubin de Teran (ed.), *Indiscreet Journeys: Stories of Women on the Road* (Faber and Faber, 1990), pp. 48–9).

48 Lesley D. Harman, *When a Hostel Becomes a Home: Experiences of Women* (Garamond Press, 1989), p. 10.

49 Janet Maslin, 'Lay off "Thelma and Louise" ', *The New York Times*, 16 June 1991.

50 *People Weekly*, 10 June 1991.

51 Susan Bordo, 'Feminism, postmodernism, and gender-scepticism', in Linda J. Nicholson (ed.), *Feminism/Postmodernism* (Routledge, 1990).

52   Elspeth Probyn, 'Travels in the postmodern: making sense of the local', in Nicholson (ed.), *Feminism/Postmodernism* (Routledge, 1990); Adrienne Rich 'Notes towards a politics of location', in *Blood, Bread, and Poetry: Selected Prose 1979–1985* (W. W. Norton, 1986).

53   Caren Kaplan, 'Deterritorializations: the rewriting of home and exile in western feminist discourse', *Cultural Critique*, no. 6 (1987).

54   Indeed, Van Den Abbeele points out that the word 'metaphor' comes from a Greek word meaning transfer or transport: *Travel as Metaphor*, p. xxii.

8

Angry Young Men and Minor (Female) Characters: The Idea of 'America' in 1950s Popular Culture

America allows you to invent a self better adjusted to the individual you have become since outgrowing the impositions of birth.

Peter Conrad[1]

For teds and other young British people, rock-'n'-roll meant the exotic excitement of the United States in a generalized version of gangsters, 'automobiles' and Hollywood . . . It was fantasized in the decor of coffee bars and juke-boxes.

Alan Sinfield[2]

The fifties . . . were a mutilating time to grow up female.

Marge Piercy[3]

Three years after I came to the United States on a one-way ticket, but before I got my green card, I was having lunch with a colleague; he was a man exactly my age, another deserter from Britain, who divides his time between Canada and the US. I tried out on him my idea that apart from the sensible reasons for crossing the Atlantic, mainly the disintegration of higher education in Britain and the far more dynamic and congenial conditions of such work in North America, some of us are also playing out a more fundamental fantasy, which has to do with growing up in Britain in the 1950s. For myself I am convinced of this, that 'America' has some deep and complex structure of meaning which was produced in my mid-teens (the late 1950s) and which for thirty years has continued to operate as a strong, if rather inarticulate fantasy, drawing me to things American and eventually bringing me to work in the United States. My friend knew exactly what I meant, and said it was just the same for him. So we talked for a while about the fifties in Britain, and about our experiences of living and working there and in North America. But then, in a sharp dislocation of our mutual understanding, it emerged that 'America' meant something quite different to each of us. For me, the fifties fantasy had to do with Hollywood movies and especially rock 'n' roll. For him it was entirely bound up with Kerouac and jazz. Elvis, Little Richard, and Eddie Cochran meant nothing to him, then or now. For my part, I agree with the view of Michael McKean (David St Hubbins of Spinal Tap) on jazz: 'I have always thought that jazz was basically people making mistakes. They start with the tune, then they go, 'Whoops!' But instead of saying whoops, they just go on and pretend like they did it on purpose.'[4]

At the time, we concluded this must be a gendered thing, jazz and 'the road' being specifically masculine preserves. I think this is partly true, though, as several women writers – novelists and memoirists – have said, it was common for women in Beat circles to attach themselves to the edges of the worlds of their men in that period.[5] But some of the women of the Beat generation in New York in the fifties also attest to a love of jazz themselves. Diane di Prima says that 'jazz was for us the most important, happening art'.[6] Hettie Jones worked for the jazz magazine *Record Changer*, hung out with jazz musicians and went to the Annual Jazz Festival at Newport, Rhode Island.[7] For others, Kerouac articulated the appeal of the road to which they too were susceptible. Jan Clausen was inspired by reading *On the Road* as a teenager in 1957.[8] Joyce Johnson and Carolyn Cassady, both of whom were involved with Kerouac himself, longed to travel with him.[9] These accounts, even though written retrospectively and, for the most part, with the irony and self-deprecation of a later feminist understanding, may not quite get at the truth of women's desires in the fifties, since, as Wini Breines puts it, 'female bohemians became beats by becoming the girlfriends of the "real" Beats',[10] hence often adopting or simulating the passions of their men. And although there are bound to be gender differences in the operation of the fantasy of 'America', I do not think it can be as simple as a dual alignment under particular cultural headings. (Apart from anything else, rock 'n' roll figured just as importantly for boys as for girls, despite my colleague's own lack of interest) As Peter Conrad says, 'the reality of America is selective, optional, fantastic: there is an America for each of us'.[11]

But there are certain persistent themes that constitute the remembered fantasy. For the most part, these may not have much to do either with the reality of life in the United States in that period or with the prevalent idea ('myth' it has more recently been called) of that reality – an ideology of consensus, of a family-centred, prosperous existence. Rather, it was always the underside of that myth which played, in both negative and positive ways, on the other side of the Atlantic. The phenomena invoked were the products of popular culture, disdained and resisted by the establishment in the United States and Britain.[12] Historians of the 1950s in the United States have shown how popular music, film and aspects of youth culture operated as a rebellion against the claustrophobic life and conservative values of that period.[13] In Britain, the dominant response to American popular culture was one of hostility, combined with a concerted effort to prevent its contamination of British culture and British youth. As Duncan Webster has shown, this fear of Americanization was not new in the 1950s; it can be traced to Matthew Arnold and Edmund Gosse in the nineteenth century, through the cultural criticism of F. R. Leavis in the 1930s.[14] (The fear was also not specifically British. Similarly negative images of America operated between the wars in Germany, where it also functioned as a contrast to the notion of 'Heimat', home, and of German identity.[15]) What Dick Hebdige has called 'the spectre of Americanisation'[16] persists to the late twentieth century, when fears about the consequences of deregulating the media have often been articulated in terms of the threat of the invasion of British television by American programmes, and a general lowering of standards to the perceived abysmal quality of the media in the United States. Webster points out that recent debates about video nasties in Britain replay the campaign against American horror comics in the 1950s.[17] But the post-war period produced its own specific conditions for a hostility to aspects of American culture, at a time when Britain was dependent on the United States (in military and then economic terms) and when Britain had lost international status as a world power relative to the United States.

At the same time, a positive mythology of 'America' was active in

Europe. For German artists in the 1920s, jazz, American dance, the modern city and an American model of rational organization were the inspiration for their work.[18] The film director Wim Wenders has written a thirty-page poem about his 'American Dream', in this case a post-war dream.

> The first thing I got to know about America
> were pictures. In comics – Mickey Mouse was my favourite –
> and magazines. We didn't have television then.
> Incredible highway junctions!
> Trees so big that cars drove through them!
> Women in bikinis! The most beautiful women
> Cars! Wild and wonderful cars, some of which would set
> world records on salt lakes!
> Aeroplanes breaking the sound barrier, twice the speed of sound!
>
> . . .
>
> And finally old enough to go to the movies.
> American films spoke more clearly about America
> than anything else had before.
> Especially the Westerns, my favourites.
>
> . . .
>
> And then, suddenly,
> overnight,
> there was a music
> that had nothing to do with the rest,
> that offered a new definition instead.
> It was called 'Rock 'n' Roll'
> and was always turned off immediately by the powers that be.
> 'Jungle music.'
> From that day on music existed.[19]

As Alan Sinfield says (in relation to the culture of post-war Britain), 'if "Americanization" was indeed cultural imperialism it was also, for the Teds and other young people, a mode of resistance . . . The use of US culture to unsettle traditional elements in the local culture is common all round the world.'[20]

Like the German artists of the 1920s, British artists who were associated with the Independent Group and the ICA in London in the 1950s quoted, promoted and used American popular culture in their work. The curators of a major exhibition of the work of this group in 1990 recall this central orientation, as well as the pervasive hostility to US culture which it was intended to overturn:

> Postwar realities ... were dominated by American technology and popular culture, including car designs, advertising, science fiction, popular music, movies, and art. The British intellectual establishment regarded this Americanization of culture with distaste. But for artists such as Richard Hamilton and Eduardo Paolozzi, for the architects Alison and Peter Smithson, and for the critics Lawrence Alloway and Reyner Banham, among others, 'America' represented the future and the unprecedented opportunities and problems presented by a new global mass culture.[21]

The new visual imagery was replete with borrowings from advertising, science fiction, the movies and mass culture, culminating in the work shown at the 1956 exhibition *This is Tomorrow*, one section of which featured the following:

> [A] sixteen-foot-high image of Robbie the Robot [from the film *Forbidden Planet*]; Marilyn Monroe, her skirt flying, in a scene from *The Seven Year Itch*; the giant bottle of Guinness; the spongy floor that, when stepped on, emitted strawberry air freshener; the optical illusion 'corridor'; the total collage effect of the "Cinemascope" panel; the jukebox; and the reproduction of van Gogh's *Sunflowers*.[22]

This borrowing was, of course, a fairly selective process. The sounds and images which found their way into European artistic and youth cultures in the 1950s were not the official culture of America, but rather its own voices of rebellion. Post-war America has been characterized by social historians as conservative and repressive, dominated by the politics and ideology of the Cold War and by supremely traditional values of family and sexuality.[23] Such social histories attempt, not very successfully, to counteract the image of the 1950s in the popular consciousness of subsequent years, which sees that decade as an idyllic time of prosperity, happy suburban family-centred existence and unproblematic law and order. This nostalgic view is sustained by daily re-runs on cable television of 1950s television sitcoms like *I Love Lucy* and *The Burns and Allen Show*.[24] But even in the seventies this nostalgia was under attack. In 1977, Douglas T. Miller and Marion Nowak published an exhaustive analysis and critique of the myth of the fifties.[25] As they put it, 'for many people the 1950s came to symbolize a golden age of innocence and simplicity, an era supposedly unruffled by riots, racial violence, Vietnam, Watergate, assassinations.' They also point out that this nostalgia was highly selective.[26] More recently, Stephanie Coontz has taken issue with fifties nostalgia in the 1990s, in particular with the persistent myth of the family at that time.[27]

According to Miller and Nowak this supposedly idyllic decade was a humourless and fearful time, a period of tensions, insecurities and enormously irresponsible acts of planning and city and road building, which had dire consequences, both social and aesthetic. Overall, they report, 'we would have preferred a decade that was less materialistic, militaristic, frightened, conformist, conservative, stuffy, trivial'.[28] Chapter by chapter, they document the real fear prevalent during the McCarthyite early fifties, the horrors of testing nuclear bombs, the rise of religion and its conservative effects, the development of the suburb and the car, the domestic constraints imposed on women. They indict the period and its values for a violent hostility to homosexuality and for its institutionalized and pervasive racism. By now, we are familiar with these charges, yet the nostalgia persists in popular memory, much like the unexamined affection for Victorian values so successfully invoked by Margaret Thatcher and other conservative politicians in the 1980s. Coontz suggests, too, that the myth of the fifties is distorted in another way, in that it obscures the *diversity* of family life even at that time. Differences of class and race throw into question the assumption that the television sitcom family, middle-class, white, suburban, was universal. And the dominant conception of the fifties family as self-contained and self-reliant manages to ignore the involvement of the state in many guises – through housing loans, education payments, social welfare and so on.[29]

The decade also produced its own forms of critique, articulated in popular culture and in the subcultural activities of young white people: the Beats, jazz, rock 'n' roll, James Dean, Marlon Brando and movies about the restlessness and rebellion of youth. Central to much of this was the discourse of race, in which 'blackness' operated as a radical signifier; social transgressions of ethnic boundaries were an important aspect of white rebellion, whether in relation to the 'black' music (r & b) which was taken over in early rock 'n' roll, or in relation to jazz and the emergence of the 'white negro'.[30] In addition, the social conditions of the period – expanded education, enhanced leisure, the large-scale migration of blacks out of the rural South and into the cities, increased employment opportunities for women – laid the foundations for youth culture, the civil rights movement and the women's movement.

The last of these, however, would not be mobilized until well into the 1960s; it was only in 1963 that Betty Friedan was able to identify the 'problem that had no name',[31] which underlay the dissatisfaction of suburban wives, bored and, frequently, tranquillized.[32] The documents of the period, only forty years later, seem prehistoric in their identification of women's role. David Halberstam quotes Mrs Dale Carnegie from *Better Homes and Gardens* in 1955: 'The two big steps that women must take are to help their husbands decide where they are going and use their pretty heads to help them get there.'[33] Countless women's magazines and pseudo-scientific texts told women that marriage and child-bearing should be their primary and sufficient goals.[34] We know now that the happy housewife of the 1950s was often extremely unhappy, and sometimes desperate.

Recalling that time however, a few white women have also recorded some of the ways they found to negotiate the gender constraints.[35] Marge Piercy, who viewed the fifties as a 'mutilating time to grow up female', identifies the only option for women in this oppressive society as one of 'wriggling through the cracks, surviving in the unguarded interstices'.[36] At a moment of apparently seamless consensus, even the dominant culture could not operate as a monolithic set of values.[37] At the simplest level, a rejection of the mother as a model for one's life constituted a mini-revolt (though one with real costs in terms of guilt, and an important topic for therapies in the 1980s and 1990s). The double bind for girls when opting for sexual freedom in the face of a gender ideology that insisted on premarital virginity meant being labelled 'slut' rather than 'rebel', but many women recall the importance of sexual experience as rebellion.[38] Breines writes about the importance of the alternative cultures (rock music, black culture, the Beats) for girls and young women independent enough to look for ways of escaping the suburban idyll.[39] Greenwich Village figures large in these escape scenarios, as a symbolic and actual place for possibilities of a different life.[40]

For some women race played a part in the struggle to overstep the boundaries. The heroines of Lynn Lauber's novel *White Girls* and of Joyce Carol Oates's *Because it is Bitter, and Because it is My Heart*, set in the 1950s and early 1960s, become obsessively involved with young black men.[41] Hettie Jones, in her own escape from suburbia, married LeRoi Jones (alienating her family and, later, in the early days of the Black Power movement, having to confront a different kind of rejection as a white woman).[42] As Breines says, 'some white girls used the sensibilities of darkness as a way out of boredom and restlessness . . . they were drawn to black music and difference – delinquent and dark boyfriends, working-class, Beat, and bohemian lovers, jazz and rock and roll – because these were inappropriate and forbidden'.[43]

But the rebellions of the 1950s were not hospitable to women. The cultures of rebellion (youth cultures, the Beats, the 'white negro') were male, sexist and most often sexually reactionary. Zane, the heroine of Alix Kates Shulman's novel, *Burning Questions*, describes the scene early in her new life in the Village:

> The room was probably filled with girls who'd come to the Village from all over on trains and busses, found rooms and jobs, and rushed straight down to the famous places on MacDougal Street. There we all were in our black tights and ponytails trying to act gutsy, though underneath our clothes we were still sweet things with the smell of the Midwest just under our skins. Not yet knowing that innocence turned some men on, we tried to hide ours under black eye makeup, rose perfume, and seductive smiles, disguising our loneliness and origins by sleeping around. Some of the men, lonely too, covered theirs by growing beards and professing Art. Art, Art, Art, they said, creating community. (I believed every word!) They carried slim notebooks in their back hip pockets to scribble in as they sat in their favorite cafe night after night and played the out-of-towners' favorite game, mutual recognition. They acted as if to belong they had only to open their notebooks; but we had to open our legs: for us, art talk and scribbling were considered pretentious.[44]

Joyce Johnson and Hettie Jones have written similar accounts, autobiographical rather than fictional, of their lives as rebels but also as secondary and vulnerable to men (Kerouac and LeRoi Jones respectively).[45] The texts of the Beats and other 1950s male rebels speak for themselves on this issue. Kerouac's famous introduction to Robert Frank's book of photographs *The Americans* eulogizes the road, waxes poetic over the images, and concludes: 'To Robert Frank I now give this message: You got eyes. / And I say: That little ole lonely elevator girl looking up sighing in an elevator full of blurred

demons, what's her name & address?'[46] White heterosexual girls
and women, engaged in the available strategies to escape their suburban fate, found themselves more the facilitators of men's rebellion,
particularly as sexual partners, than equal participants in personal
and social transformation. As Johnson says, they were 'minor characters' in the drama of the Beat generation.[47]

The story of the 1950s in England is similar, but also crucially
different. Post-war Britain was radically changed from its pre-war
status and character by virtue of two important developments: its
decline as a world power relative to the United States and its domestic transformation into a welfare state.[48] Although the post-war
Labour government was short-lived (ceding power in 1951 to the
Conservatives and thirteen years of Tory rule) the succeeding admin-
istrations were also welfarist; most of the social and economic changes
put into place during its tenure were not to be dismantled until the
1980s. These included state intervention in the economy, the nation-
alization of certain important sectors, the development of a national
health service, and the development and expansion of public service
broadcasting[49] and of a system of state support for the arts (the Arts
Council of Great Britain was established in 1945). In addition, the
Labour party came to power in 1945 while stating in its manifesto:
'The Labour Party is a Socialist Party and proud of it. Its ultimate
aim is the establishment of the Socialist Commonwealth of Great
Britain.'[50] Such rhetoric and such politics would have been unthinkable in American politics at the time, as it has of course become
unthinkable in British politics in the last fifteen years, though it is
important not to overstate the differences. As Elizabeth Wilson says,
'in the fifties Britain was a conservative society described in the
rhetoric of a radical ideology'.[51] Nevertheless, although Britain was
an active participant in the Cold War, there was far more room for
manoeuvre for radicals, who aligned themselves with CND, the
Communist Party (at least until 1956), and the New Left and its
journals later in the decade.

The experience and politics of race relations were very different in
Britain and the United States in this period. It was only in the 1950s
that immigration into Britain from the soon-to-be-independent colo-
nies began on a substantial scale.[52] London Transport then actively
recruited in the Caribbean and, until the introduction of restrictive
immigration measures in the 1960s and later, migration from the
Indian subcontinent, from African countries and from the Caribbean

accelerated considerably.[53] The immigrants confronted institutional and social racism, just as blacks and other minorities had always done in the United States. But the absence of a history of clear racial divisions in pre-war Britain meant that 'blackness' did not signify culturally in the same way, having more to do with the colonial 'other' and with the exotic. So, for example, Sinfield points out that, unlike in the United States, in Britain the black dimension of rock 'n' roll was absent and therefore would not register to an audience unaware of its origins and unfamiliar with the black radio stations that had played the music which had preceded and informed it.[54] It also meant that for men and women in Britain in the 1950s racial transgression was unlikely to operate as a strategy of rebellion in the way it could do in America.

Revolt in Britain accordingly took different forms. It is most readily associated with certain intellectuals,[55] notably the so-called Angry Young Men of literature and theatre, and with the first post-war youth cultures, especially the working-class Teddy boys, who gained a reputation for wrecking cinemas and general hooliganism.[56] Forms of rebellion, as always, varied according to class, education and political sympathy. In the case of left-wing intellectuals and artists associated with the ICA and the Independent Group, one focus for cultural radicalism was the 1951 Festival of Britain, which was perceived as self-satisfied, conservative and backward looking.[57] The literary texts of revolt expressed a more diffuse dissatisfaction, sometimes formulated in terms of class resentment (John Osborne's play *Look Back in Anger* of 1956, John Braine's *Room at the Top* of 1957, Kingsley Amis's *Lucky Jim* of 1954, Alan Sillitoe's *Saturday Night and Sunday Morning* of 1958), sometimes as a generic existential angst (Colin Wilson's treatise, *The Outsider*, of 1956). Youth cultures were a different phenomenon, whether the more visible working-class variant of the Teddy boys or the less articulated activities and preferences of the young people who were beginning to use styles of dress and types of music to shape identities for themselves.

Where are the women in this scenario of revolt? It is notorious that *Look Back in Anger* expresses its class rage through the emotional battering of a middle-class woman.[58] In fact, the texts of the Angry Young Men are pervaded, almost without exception, by a rampant misogyny. Nor did women play an important part in any of the cultures of rebellion of that decade. The architect Alison

Smithson, a member of the Independent Group, stands out as a rare woman prominent in fifties culture. The critic Lawrence Alloway, a founder member of the Group, notes in retrospect: 'It must be admitted that the IG possessed a male chauvinist streak more to be tolerated in the 1950s in Great Britain than elsewhere: the women in the group were without exception wives and girl friends.'[59] Tom Maschler's contemporary collection of the words and thoughts of the Angry Young Men, published in 1958, included only one woman, Doris Lessing.[60] Like their counterparts in the United States, women in Britain were not only excluded from or marginal to the rebellion of men: they were often the *object* of the anger, the primary victim of the revolt. Lynne Segal has explored the crisis of masculinity in Britain in the 1950s, showing that the literal domestication of men (that is the social transformations and ideologies which emphasized a new family-based existence, as in the States), combined with the end of the war and the decline of national military service, produced this crisis, acted out in terms of homophobia and misogyny.[61] It is necessary to understand the gendered and radically unequal nature of cultural rebellion in the light of this.

The lives of women in Britain in the 1950s were in many ways similar to those of women in the United States. The new ideology of family life, though perhaps not as insistently promoted, was also in effect in Britain. Although many women were taking jobs outside the home, especially part-time jobs, the primary emphasis was on women's domestic roles as wives and mothers.[62] The Welfare State made little difference to the domestic tasks and obligations assigned to women.[63] The education of girls, too, was premised on the assumption that domesticity was their goal.[64] Mary Evans has recalled the experience of an education in a girls' grammar school in that period:

> The responsibilities of the housewife and the mother were given full credit by the staff and 'making a home' was an ideal which was accorded full status by a staff that was largely unmarried. So having a 'working' mother was regarded as slightly peculiar, and rather eccentric. . . . When the school debated the issue that 'A Woman's Place is in the Home' the school decided that this was certainly the case.[65]

Other women remembering the 1950s recall the ways, limited though they were, in which they resisted the inculcation of a monolithic femininity. Harriet Gilbert, after a childhood of training to give up ungirlish things, performed her own mini-rebellion by rejecting university, the next step in her family's imagined trajectory for the dutiful daughter, in favour of drama school.[66] Valerie Walkerdine looks back on school years of excellent school reports and a career as a 'steady, reliable worker', after which she found herself quite unable to study at college, but energized by 'the desperate avoidance of what was expected by so many other would-be teachers: the engagement ring and return to the provinces to marry'.[67] Elements of youth and counter culture are taken up: Stef Pixner frequents an expresso bar, sitting at black tables and hoping to meet boys.[68] Alison Fell and Sheila Rowbotham, in Scotland and the north of England, listen to Elvis and to British pop singers.[69] Liz Heron, the editor of these memoirs, suggests that girls in the fifties 'had a stronger sense of our possibilities than the myths about the fifties allow',[70] partly because they were products of the Welfare State (many of the contributors to the volume mention free orange juice, cod-liver oil and school milk), and partly because of the lingering war-time image of women's independence and confidence. This notion that girls of the period inherited a sense of 'a right to the earth'[71] is part of the explanation for the later articulation of an explicitly feminist consciousness among these same women.

I read these accounts of the 1950s, recognizing some things and not others. Geographical and class differences inflect their accounts.[72] I recognize the syndrome of the steady, reliable worker, always top in class, and the minimal rebellion of rejecting university (in my case to become a secretary). I remember the first coffee bars in Manchester – the Mogambo and the Mokarlo I think – though not much about what went on in them. Mostly, I remember the music, and listening to Radio Luxembourg at night, and beginning to fantasize 'America'. Nothing of this is present in these other memoirs, however, and I begin to wonder whether just as 'America' can mean different things to different people, the same applies to the fifties. Evans says none of her contemporaries had any interest in the United States, which 'remained largely foreign, a rather crass country glimpsed more or less entirely though the advertisements in the *National Geographic* magazine', a place which they would not want to visit, since 'the United States would not be interesting as it "had no history".'[73] None of the contributors to Heron's collection of memoirs mentions America – or 'America'. Worse, some of those who do mention rock music favour the sanitized British covers of American songs. Rowbotham found Elvis too scary, and proclaims 'my heart was given to Tommy Steele', a non-rock 'n' roller of the first order.[74] Alison Fell listens to Cliff Richard, but at least she prefers 'wild Elvis' (and secretly wants to be him).[75] Of the various fifties fantasies I have discussed here, mine seems to have most in common with that of Wenders – a German and a man – for whom the idea of a new identity was created by the possibilities inherent in American music and American culture (and for whom, too, this eventually had to be followed up by actually going to the United States).

The first chapter in this book considered the way in which geographically distant places can operate as liberating fantasies and facilitating locations in the project of forming an identity, particularly for women. There is no doubt that 'America' has played this role for many Europeans, male and female. In Britain in the 1950s its meaning was both historically specific and fluid enough to be available for many varied co-optations. 'America' signified economic and military power, classlessness, suburban family life, philistine culture and lack of history, the excitement of new, transgressive cultural forms (jazz, dance, rock 'n' roll, movies). It is not surprising, then, that my colleague and I discovered that our individual fantasies were so at variance. It is also clear that oppositional cultures and the fantasies that inform them do not work in any simple gender-specific way. Nevertheless, just as lives, experiences and possibilities for men and women differed greatly in the 1950s, both in Britain and in the US, so did their forms of counter-culture and revolt. At the moment, we know most about the cultures of rebellion of men in that period, since women were indeed only minor characters in those scenes. Now that more women on both sides of the Atlantic have begun to write a different history of fifties adolescence and youth, these stories have to be revised. It would be wrong, of course, to employ a later feminist consciousness when looking at a period in which, for the most part, women were quite unaware of their subservience to male culture and unable to articulate, except retrospectively, their unease and dissatisfaction with this state of affairs. Nevertheless, the strategies girls and women found to negotiate their oppression, to manoeuvre 'through the cracks', also laid the foundations for the feminism of the late 1960s. In the 1950s, young white women as well as young white men were engaged in the struggle for identity in the face of official constructions of femininity and masculinity. On the one hand the decade confronted us with one of the most insistent and closed models for behaviour and for a possible future; on the other it showed us there were real possibilities for something different. Aspects of popular, often forbidden, culture helped many of us to articulate those possibilities. In my case (and both of these things I share with other fifties survivors, though not with all of them) primary among these was rock 'n' roll (but only American rock 'n' roll) and a diffuse fantasy of 'America' as a site, as Conrad says, of a potential self.

NOTES

1   Peter Conrad, *Imagining America* (Avon Books, 1980), p. 5.
2   Alan Sinfield, *Literature, Politics, and Culture in Postwar Britain* (University of California Press, 1989), pp. 152–3.
3   Marge Piercy, 'Through the cracks: growing up in the fifties', in *Parti-Colored Blocks for a Quilt* (University of Michigan Press, 1982), p. 126.
4   *New York Times*, 15 March 1992.
5   See, for example, Alix Kates Shulman, *Burning Questions* (Thunder's Mouth Press, 1990 [1978]); Joyce Johnson, *Minor Characters* (Picador, 1983); Hettie Jones, *How I Became Hettie Jones* (E. P. Dutton, 1990).
6   Diane di Prima, *Memoirs of a Beatnik* (Last Gasp, 1988 [1969]), p. 93.
7   Jones, *How I became Hettie Jones*, pp. 16–17, 30–1.
8   Jan Clausen, *Sinking Stealing* (Crossing Press, 1985), p. 146, quoted in Wini Breines, *Young, White, and Miserable: Growing up Female in the Fifties* (Beacon Press, 1992), pp. 137–8. Jack Kerouac, *On the Road* (Signet Books, New American Library, 1957).
9   Johnson, *Minor Characters*; Carolyn Cassady, *Off the Road: My Years with Cassady, Kerouac, and Ginsberg* (Wm Morrow, 1990).
10 Breines, *Young, White, and Miserable*, p. 143.
11 Conrad, *Imagining America*, p. 4.
12 But here is an exception: Brian Bedford, a British actor now in his late fifties, who emigrated to the United States in 1959, cites the appeal of 'consensus' America as well as its unofficial popular cultural forms: 'During the war, my American cousin sent me parcels of chewing gum and movie magazines, and this fired my enthusiasm. I've always been an avid movie-goer and, strangely enough, my favorites were these very domestic Doris Day movies – I was fascinated by the kitchens and the whole aura of American suburban life.' (*New York Times*, Sunday, 24 October 1993.)

13 See Douglas T. Miller and Marion Nowak, *The Fifties: The Way We Really Were* (Doubleday, 1977), especially chs 11 and 12, on music and film. Stephanie Coontz, *The Way We Never Were: American Families and the Nostalgia Trap* (Basic Books, 1992) argues that the 1950s family model, grounded as it was in consumerism, 'contained the seeds of its own destruction' (p. 38) in the youth market and in the saturation of advertising with sex. David Halberstam devotes a chapter to discussing the importance of Elvis Presley, Marlon Brando and James Dean as 'the start of a revolution': *The Fifties* (Villard Books, 1993), p. 456.

14 Duncan Webster, *Looka Yonder! The Imaginary America of Populist Culture* (Comedia/Routledge, 1988), pp. 179–83.

15 See the catalogue, *Envisioning America: Prints, Drawings, and Photographs by George Grosz and his Contemporaries 1915–1933* (Busch-Reisinger Museum, Harvard University, 1990); David Morley and Kevin Robins, 'No place like *Heimat*: Images of home(land) in European culture', *New Formations*, no. 12 (Winter 1990).

16 Dick Hebdige, 'Towards a cartography of taste 1935–1962', in *Hiding in the Light: On Images and Things* (Comedia/Routledge, 1988), p. 52.

17 Webster, *Looka Yonder!*, p. 191.

18 See the essays in *Envisioning America*.

19 Wim Wenders, 'The American Dream', in *Emotion Pictures: Reflections on the Cinema* (Faber and Faber, 1989), pp. 123–5.

20 Sinfield, *Literature, Politics, and Culture*, p. 156.

21 *The Independent Group: Postwar Britain and the Aesthetics of Plenty*, an exhibition organized by the Hood Museum of Art, Dartmouth College, and shown at various locations between 1 February 1990 and 16 August 1991: Foreword to the Catalogue (The Regents of the University of California, 1990), p. 6. On the 'Americanophilia' of British artists in the late 1950s and early 1960s, see also the essays in the catalogue *The Sixties Art Scene in London* (Barbican Art Gallery, London, 1993).

22 *The Independent Group*, p. 139. The very up-to-dateness of the work of the IG rendered its later exhibition somewhat disappointing. Seeing the show in Buffalo in 1991, I was mainly struck by how *obsolete* and naive it seemed. The trouble with working with mass cultural forms and especially contemporary technologies is that they are bound to date so quickly, something that may not have been so predictable in the 1950s, before the pace of technological development accelerated.

23 See Halberstam, *The Fifties*; Miller and Nowak, *The Fifties*; Coontz, *The Way We Never Were*.

24 For an analysis of how sitcoms worked at the time to naturalize women's place in the home, see Mary Beth Haralovich, 'Sitcoms and suburbs:

positioning the 1950s homemaker', *Quarterly Review of Film and Video*, vol. 11, no. 1 (1989).

25 Miller and Nowak, *The Fifties*.

26 Ibid., p. 5.

27 Coontz, *The Way We Never Were*.

28 Miller and Nowak, *The Fifties*, p. 12.

29 Coontz, *The Way We Never Were*, pp. 29–31, 76–91.

30 On this category, see Andrew Ross, 'Hip, and the long front of color', in *No Respect: Intellectuals and Popular Culture* (Routledge, 1989).

31 Betty Friedan, *The Feminine Mystique* (Dell, 1963).

32 Miller and Nowak, *The Fifties*, p. 138; Coontz, *The Way We Never Were*, p. 36.

33 Halberstam, *The Fifties*, pp. 591–2.

34 Miller and Nowak quote at length an influential book of 1947, which states: 'All mature childless women are . . . emotionally disturbed (as cause, or effect or both) in some fashion, whatever the reason for childlessness.' Miller and Nowak, *The Fifties*, p. 155, citing Marynia Farnham and Ferdinand Lundberg, *Modern Woman: The Lost Sex* (New York, 1947).

35 See Brett Harvey, *The Fifties: A Women's Oral History* (Harper-Collins, 1993), based on interviews with ninety-two women who were in their late teens to mid-twenties in the 1950s, which records a hidden history of abortions, struggles to remain in higher education, conflicts over sexual desire in a hypocritical culture of double-standards, and lesbian life-styles.

36 Piercy, 'Through the cracks', p. 116.

37 Jackie Byars has discussed the place of gender in 1950s melodrama films, arguing that they, while operating in primarily conservative ways to place women in the domestic sphere, also manifest internal contradictions, through which resisting voices can be heard, registering other possibilities for women's lives: *All That Hollywood Allows: Re-reading Gender in 1950s Melodrama* (The University of North Carolina Press, 1991).

38 See Harvey, *The Fifties*; Breines, *Young, White, and Miserable*; di Prima, *Memoirs of a Beatnik*. For women's recollections of the 1950s in Britain, see the essays in Liz Heron (ed.), *Truth, Dare or Promise: Girls Growing Up in the Fifties* (Virago, 1985).

39 Breines, *Young, White, and Miserable*.

40 See Johnson, *Minor Characters*; di Prima, *Memoirs of a Beatnik*; Jones, *How I Became Hettie Jones*; Shulman, *Burning Questions*.

41 Lynn Lauber, *White Girls* (W. W. Norton, 1990); Joyce Carol Oates, *Because it is Bitter, and Because it is My Heart* (Penguin, 1991).

42 Jones, *How I Became Hettie Jones*.

43 Breines, *Young, White, and Miserable*, p. 19.

44 Schulman, *Burning Questions*, pp. 97–8.
45 Johnson, *Minor Characters*; Jones, *How I Became Hettie Jones*.
46 Jack Kerouac, Introduction to *The Americans: Photographs by Robert Frank* (Museum of Modern Art, New York, 1968 [1959]), p. vi.
47 Johnson, *Minor Characters*.
48 See Elizabeth Wilson, *Only Halfway to Paradise: Women in Postwar Britain: 1945–1968* (Tavistock Publications 1980); Sinfield, *Literature, Politics, and Culture*.
49 See John Corner, 'General introduction: television and British society in the 1950s', in his edited volume, *Popular Television in Britain: Studies in Cultural History* (BFI Publishing, 1991).
50 Quoted in Sinfield, *Literature, Politics and Culture*, p. 15.
51 Wilson, *Only Halfway to Paradise*, p. 6.
52 Caryl Phillips, the British-Caribbean writer, has pointed out that for many people in England their first experience of black people was their encounter with black GIs from the US who were stationed in Britain in the 1940s. (He made this point in a talk at the New York University Creative Writing Program Reading Series, 5 November 1993.) Paul Gilroy also suggests that the dance floor provided an early meeting place for some young blacks and whites, 'long before the advent of "rock 'n' roll", the rise of soul, disco and reggae', though his study of the discourses of race and racism also focuses on the period since the 1950s, and particularly the 1970s and 1980s: *'There Ain't no Black in the Union Jack': The Cultural Politics of Race and Nation* (Hutchinson, 1987), p. 163.
53 See Sinfield, *Literature, Politics and Culture*, pp. 125–7.
54 Ibid., pp. 152–3. See also Ross's comment that 'for British musicians, raised in a culture that would not have to begin to properly acknowledge its multiracial constituency for another decade, blues music represented an exotic taste, not a lived experience for a racial minority': 'Hip, and the long front of color', p. 95.
55 This was at a time when American intellectuals were, on the whole, integrated into the consensus politics and society. See Miller and Nowak, *The Fifties*, pp. 220–47.
56 The cinema incidents were blamed on rock 'n' roll because they occurred at showings of *Blackboard Jungle* in 1955 and *Rock Around the Clock* in 1956, both of which featured music by Bill Haley.
57 *The Independent Group*, p. 16.
58 See Michelene Wandor, *Look Back in Gender: Sexuality and the Family in Post-War British Drama* (Methuen, 1987), pp. 8–14, for a discussion of how this misogyny works in relation to the male search for identity.
59 Introductory Notes in *The Independent Group*, p. 50.

60   Tom Maschler (ed.), *Declaration* (McGibbon and Kee, 1959). The men are Lindsay Anderson, Kenneth Tynan, Stuart Holroyd, John Osborne, Colin Wilson, Bill Hopkins and John Wain. There is an unexplained difference between two editions of this book: in the 1958 New York edition Doris Lessing's essay is last in order; in the 1959 London edition it is brought to the front. Belated regret at the marginalization of women in what presents itself as an important cultural document somehow seems unlikely among that company, however.

61   Lynne Segal, 'Look back in anger: men in the fifties', in Rowena Chapman and Jonathan Rutherford (eds), *Male Order: Unwrapping Masculinity* (Lawrence & Wishart, 1988).

62   See Wilson, *Only Halfway to Paradise*, chs 2–4.

63   Wilson quotes a *Daily Telegraph* journalist in 1956: 'The welfare state is based on the drudgery of women': *Only Halfway to Paradise*, p. 30.

64   Ibid., pp. 32–6.

65   Mary Evans, *A Good School: Life at a Girls' Grammar School in the 1950s* (The Women's Press, 1991), p. 29.

66   Harriet Gilbert, 'Growing Pains', in Heron (ed.), *Truth, Dare or Promise*, p. 59.

67   Valerie Walkerdine, 'Dreams from an ordinary childhood', in Heron (ed.), *Truth, Dare or Promise*, pp. 71, 76.

68   Stef Pixner, 'The oyster and the shadow', in Heron (ed.), *Truth, Dare or Promise*, p. 95.

69   Alison Fell, 'Rebel with a cause', p. 21; Sheila Rowbotham, 'Revolt in Roundhay', p. 198: both in Heron (ed.), *Truth, Dare or Promise*.

70   Heron (ed.), *Truth, Dare or Promise*, p. 6.

71   See Carolyn Steedman, 'Landscape for a good woman', in Heron (ed.), *Truth, Dare or Promise*, p. 119.

72   In terms of real memories, I am closest to Julia Pascal, who grew up in Manchester and Blackpool. Like her, I remember being bused to a place for kosher school lunch with the other Jewish children, even though my family was not particularly kosher, and passing every day the big chalked sign 'Save the Rosenbergs' (and sharing her feeling – 'I wonder who they are and hope they will be saved'). Julia Pascal, 'Prima ballerina assoluta', in Heron (ed.), *Truth, Dare or Promise*, pp. 39, 35.

73   Evans, *A Good School*, p. 33.

74   Rowbotham, 'Revolt in Roundhay', p. 198.

75   Fell, 'Rebel with a cause', p. 21.

Index